Alfred Kappes

Mother Goose's Melodies

Songs for the Nursery

Alfred Kappes

Mother Goose's Melodies
Songs for the Nursery

ISBN/EAN: 9783337181994

Printed in Europe, USA, Canada, Australia, Japan

Cover: Foto ©Thomas Meinert / pixelio.de

More available books at **www.hansebooks.com**

Mother Goose's

Melodies

OR

SONGS FOR THE NURSERY

WITH ILLUSTRATIONS IN COLOR
BY
ALFRED KAPPES

" UNCONSIDERED TRIFLES." — *Shakespeare*

BOSTON
HOUGHTON, OSGOOD AND COMPANY
The Riverside Press, Cambridge
1879

RIVERSIDE, CAMBRIDGE :
STEREOTYPED AND PRINTED BY
H. O. HOUGHTON AND COMPANY.

Of the many who must recollect the nursery jingles of their youth, how few in number are those who have ever suspected their immense age, or that they were ever more than unmeaning nonsense; far less that their creation belongs to a period before that at which the authentic records of our history commence. Yet there is no exaggeration in such a statement. We find the same trifles which erewhile lulled or amused the English infant are current in slightly varied forms throughout the North of Europe; we know that they have been sung in the northern countries for centuries, and that there has been no modern outlet for their dissemination across the German Ocean. The most natural inference is to adopt the theory of a Teutonic origin, and thus give to every genuine child-rhyme found in England and Sweden an immense antiquity. There is nothing improbable in the supposition, for the preservation of the relics of primitive literature often bears an inverse ratio to their importance.

Having . . . shown that the nursery has an archæology, the study of which may eventually lead to important results, the jingles and songs of our childhood are defended from the imputation of excessive frivolity. HALLIWELL.

To

JOHN FLEET ELIOT,

THE GREAT-GREAT-GRANDSON OF ELIZABETH GOOSE,

KNOWN WHEREVER THE ENGLISH LANGUAGE IS SPOKEN AS

MOTHER GOOSE,

This Collection of her Melodies

IS INSCRIBED,

AS AN ACKNOWLEDGMENT OF HIS KINDNESS IN SUPPLYING THE MATERIALS FROM
WHICH THE ACCOUNT OF HIS AND HER FAMILY HAS BEEN DERIVED.

PREFACE.

About the year 1856, a gentleman of Boston, a member of the Massachusetts Historical Society, while examining a file of old newspapers in the Library of the American Antiquarian Society, at Worcester, came across a dilapidated copy of the original edition of "Mother Goose's Melodies." Not more than twelve or fifteen pages were left, but, as the price was only "two coppers," it is not probable that there were many more. Being in search of other matter, he merely took note of the title and general condition and character of the work, intending to make a further examination of it at another time. Whether he ever did so is not known. His health being impaired, he soon after went to Europe, where he remained for many months.

It was not until some time after his death, which occurred in 1859, that these and certain other facts became known to the editor, who at once determined to find the book, if possible, and reprint it as a literary curiosity, with notes and a sketch of the venerable lady whose name is part and parcel of its world-wide fame. At his instance, the Assistant Librarian of the Antiquarian Society very kindly made a protracted search for the book itself, or

for any notice of it in the newspapers of the time, but without suc-
cess. Whether it has been lost, or stolen, or overlooked, is uncer-
tain ; but of the fact that the gentleman referred to discovered an
imperfect copy of the veritable *editio princeps* there can be no
doubt.

Failing to recover this copy, the editor still thought it desirable
to publish an annotated compilation of traditional nursery melodies,
together with an account of Mother Goose and her family. In
doing so, he has taken as the basis of his work Halliwell's well-
known and excellent collection of the "Nursery Rhymes of England;" but he has omitted not a few of the pieces contained in
that collection, chiefly such as have become obsolete, or are dia-
lectical, or of merely local currency. On the other hand, he has
added from various sources a number which are familiar to American children, and are doubtless, equally with the others, relics that
have come down to us from a former age.

Of the notes, some are historical, others explanatory, and others
again merely illustrative. Most of the former are taken from Halliwell's book, already named, or from his "Popular Rhymes and
Nursery Tales," which forms a pendant or sequel to it; and his
language has been retained or modified as seemed desirable in each
instance. The facts related in them rest primarily on his authority,
although his statements have been verified wherever it was possible
to do so.

The introductory account of ' The Goose or Vergoose Family "
— which contains a notice of " Mother Goose," the putative author
of the " Melodies," and of Thomas Fleet, the compiler and publisher
of them — has mainly been prepared from materials collected by

a lineal descendant of both those worthies, and by him kindly placed at the disposal of the editor.

Not only is the name of Mother Goose a household word throughout America, but wherever the Yankee has gone — and he has penetrated to the uttermost parts of the earth — Mother Goose has gone with him. In England, however, she has never become thoroughly naturalized, or rather she seems to have lost her identity, and been transmogrified into the old woman who in modern times has been made the mother of the boy who has taken the place of the man who, in Æsop's fable, owned the goose that laid golden eggs! (See pages 87, 181.) In this character she has acquired a degree of celebrity that is largely owing to a very popular pantomime by Thomas Dibdin, called " Mother Goose, or the Golden Egg," which was brought out at Covent Garden in 1806, and had a run of ninety-two nights. As poetess laureate to the nursery she is less known there. Halliwell has nothing whatever to say about her, and no English bibliographical work contains her name. At least, it is not mentioned, as far as the writer knows, in any catalogue of chap-books, garlands, and popular histories, or of old or rare books, or the like.

It is a singular fact, that, in 1697, — twenty-two years before the Melodies were given to the world by Fleet, — Charles Perrault should have published (under the name of his infant son, Perrault d'Armancourt) a collection of fairy tales, under the title of " Contes de ma Mère l'Oye," that is, Tales of my Mother Goose. But the coincidence, though very curious, seems to have been purely accidental. Perrault's reason for adopting this title is thus explained by Collin de Plancy: —

" King Robert II. of France took to wife his relative Bertha, but was commanded by Pope Gregory V. to relinquish her, and to perform a seven years' penance for marrying within the forbidden degrees of consanguinity. Being excommunicated for disobeying the command, and his kingdom laid under an interdict, everybody forsook him except two servants. Not long after, his wife having been confined, a *lusus naturæ*, somewhat resembling a deformed duck, or, as some say, a goose, was shown him, and declared to be the offspring to which she had given birth. The king, struck with horror, repudiated Bertha, and subsequently married Constance [a daughter of Guillaume Taillefer, Count of Toulouse]. It was further asserted that Bertha had one foot shaped like that of a goose, and the credulous populace — remembering how the wife of Pepin the Short was named 'Bertha with the great foot,' because one foot was larger than the other — called the divorced wife of their unhappy king, 'Goose-footed Bertha' and 'Queen Goose.' The French have a proverbial saying that any incredible tale belongs to 'the time when Queen Bertha spun,' and they call such a tale 'one of Queen Goose's, or Mother Goose's stories.' Now, in all the vignettes which accompany the old editions of Perrault's 'Contes de ma Mère l'Oye,' 'Mother Goose' is represented as using a distaff, and as surrounded with a group of children, whom she holds entranced by her wondrous tales."

From this account it will be seen that there is no connection between the name of the imaginary relater of Perrault's fairy tales and that of the old lady whose verses ravished our infancy. Indeed it may well be doubted whether our Mother Goose or her publisher ever heard of their French contemporary.

In sending out this little anthology of "*unconsidered* trifles," the editor is aware that Mr. Gradgrind will censure him for his indifference to the realities and facts and calculations which are the proper pabulum of the infant mind, and will accuse him of aspiring

"To suckle fools and chronicle small beer;"

but he is content to submit the book to the verdict of the nursery and of those "children of a larger growth" for whom the associations connected with the nursery have not lost all their charm.

The Publishers have taken advantage of a new issue of this work to present to the public some admirable designs in color by Mr. Alfred Kappes, which they think need no commendation. In other respects the edition has been improved and embellished.

THE nobility of the goose is not so obvious as that of the swan. Yet [the word] was in ancient and honorable use as a man's name. Genseric, the name of the great Vandal chief, is referred by Grimm to *gänserich*, a gander. But it was no doubt the wild goose which gave the name, and, if we consider, we shall see that this bird has some qualities calculated to command the respect of these early roving tribes. A powerful bird, strong on the wing, taking long flights to distant lands, marshalled with the most beautiful discipline of instinct, it formed no inapt emblem of those migratory plunderers who renewed their unwelcome visitations with each succeeding Spring.

FERGUSON.

THE GOOSE OR VERGOOSE FAMILY.

MOTHER GOOSE — clarum et venerabile nomen — is not an imaginary personage, as is commonly supposed. She was born, lived, and died at a good old age in Boston, Massachusetts. Although no "blue blood" ran in her veins, the family to which she belonged was respectable and proverbially wealthy. They came from England, but at what time they alighted on these shores is not known. It is certain, however, that they had established themselves in Boston, and held real estate there as early as 1659. The name first appears on record in 1660. It occurs at different times under the forms of Goose, Vergoose, and — in one document — Vertigoose. The last two seem to be hybrids, and are perhaps of Anglo Norman origin. If so, they probably signify *green goose*, that is, a goose less than four months old, *ver* being an old Norman-French form of the modern French word *vert*, meaning *green*. The simpler, and primitive form of *Goose* was in use as a personal name in very ancient times ; and it is not yet extinct. The London Directory for 1867 has it, and it is not unusual in East Anglia, but Boston knows it no more, the last of the race that bore the illustrious cognomen having died in the year 1807.

In the 4th book in the Registry of Deeds Office of the County of Suffolk, there is a "deed of sale" from one Anthony Harker, who, in consideration of the sum of £30, money in hand, paid by Peter Vergoose, of Boston, yeoman, in behalf of his son Isaac Vergoose, conveys to the said Isaac his "old dwelling house with the one clear mojety or one halfe part of the yard orchard & Land thereto belonging as it is scittuated lying & being in Boston & being thirty fower foote at each end more or Lesse and is bounded by the streete Leading to Roxbury on the East." This deed is dated March 23, 1659–60. Immediately following this, on the next page of the same book, is a quitclaim deed, dated January 12, 1661-62, from Peter Vertigoose to Isaac Vertigoose, from which it appears that Isaac Vertigoose (or Vergoose, or Goose), when he became twenty-one years of age (which was about 1658), was desirous of bettering his condition by going to sea, or in some other way, but Peter, his father, "growing into yeares," needed assistance in his business, which was that of a "ship joyner," and wishing also to place him in a more eligible situation, agreed to give him the sum of "tenn pounds yearely" and the quitclaim of the estate above mentioned, as compensation for remaining at home.

Five years after this — that is, in 1667 — Peter died, his age unknown. The inventory of his "goods and chattels, housen and lands," amounted to £193 9s., of which the dwelling-house, garden, and cow-house were valued at £60. The precise location of the dwelling-house is not stated, but the description given in the document of sale, shows that it was on Newbury Street (now Washington Street), opposite what is now Avon Street, adjoining southerly on Anthony Harker. In the division of the estate, Susannah, the widow, had 42 feet, Harker 34 feet, and Isaac, the son, 34 feet 6 inches, making the whole front 110 feet 6 inches. The lot was 275 feet deep, and included a large part of what is now Temple Place.

In 1679, Susannah Vergoose, in consideration of the sum of £50 paid in hand, and of £15 annually during her life, conveyed to her son Isaac a piece of land bounded by land of Harker and others on the street or highway leading to Roxbury. She occupied the old house, and died there in 1685, age not known. Her inventory, which is on record, amounted to £95 1s. Her will is also on record, dated December 23, 1681. Besides her son Isaac, already mentioned, she had a daughter, who married John Raynesford, and another son, Peter, who lived in Norwich, England, the place from which the family originally came.

Isaac Vergoose, otherwise Goose, was thirty-eight years of age when he became the chief of his tribe. He was an active, enterprising man, and accumulated what in those days was considered to be a large property. In the inventory of his estate, his "housen and land" are valued at £650. He was twice married. His first wife was Mary Balston, daughter of Jonathan Balston, a well-to-do shipwright, who lived at the foot of Milk Street, near Fort Hill. To her he was married in 1667 or thereabouts. She died in 1690, aged 42 years, having borne to him ten children. Her grave-stone and those of two of her children are to be seen in the old Granary burying ground on Tremont Street. Dissatisfied with the loneliness of widowerhood, Isaac, notwithstanding his large family of boys and girls — perhaps because of his large family, — got married again, on the 5th of July, 1692, the ceremony being performed "by James Russell, assistant." His "second wentur" was Elizabeth Foster, the immortal "MOTHER GOOSE." She was a daughter of William and Ann Foster of Charlestown, and was born April 5, 1665. At the time of her marriage, therefore, she was 27 years of age, her husband being about 55. She became the mother of at least six children. No others are recorded, but it is not at all unlikely that there were others, for the records about this time are very imperfect. As she was also stepmother to the children by the first wife, one is half inclined to believe that to these facts we owe the famous rhyme about the

"old woman who lived in a shoe.
She had so many children she didn't know what to do."

Isaac Vergoose died November 29, 1710, aged 73 years. His will is dated May 9, 1710, and was recorded March 14, 1711. By it his wife Elizabeth was constituted sole executrix, and to her he gave one third part of all his real estate during her natural life; and all his household goods, personal estate, and movables of every kind forever. To his surviving children by his first wife, he gave his "Pasture Land scituate in Essex Street." This lot measured 300 feet on Essex Street, and included the land on which the Essex Street Church and the Rowe Street Baptist Church lately stood. To his four surviving children by his second wife — namely, Elizabeth, Ann, Isaac, and Peter, — he gave "All the rest & residue" of his "houses and Lands wheresoever & whatsoever, to be Equally Divided amongst them," when his youngest child should "arrive to full age"; also, his "Wife's Thirds therein for Life at and after her Decease." "And in case any of my four last named Children," says the will, "Dye within Age, the survivours to enjoy ye part of the deceased in proportion as afores^d." "J give and bequeath Two third parts of the Rents Jncome and profits of my said housing and Lands to my said four last named Children during their Minority for their Support and maintenance And if the profits and Jncomes of my said Estate be not Sufficient for that End Then J do fully Authorize and empower my said wife Elisabeth . . . to make Sale of any part of my housing and Lands to that use and to Execute good and Sufficient Deeds for the same." The whole estate was appraised at £829 4s. 10d. But Isaac was like the goose that laid the golden eggs; no addition was made to his property after his death.

The children of Isaac and Elizabeth Vergoose were —

1. Elizabeth, born May 5, 1693, died May 20, 1693.
2. Elizabeth, born May 27, 1694, died 1775.
3. Ann, born July 1, 1696, died young.
4. Isaac, born 1692 (living in 1796).
5. Ann, born May, 1703, died 1774.
6. Peter, born July 7, 1708, died after 1734 or 5.

In the record of marriages in the City Registrar's office may be found this entry | Thomas Fleet | Elizth Goose | Rev. Dr Cotton Mather Presby^e. | June 8, 1715 | This Elizabeth was the second of those whose names are given in the preceding list. Thomas Fleet was a son of Thomas and Isabella Fleet, of Tilstock, a chapelry in the parish of Whitchurch, Shropshire, England. He was born in that place September 8, 1685. When he had grown to be a lad, he was apprenticed to a printer in Bristol, and afterwards worked there as a journeyman. While he was employed there in that capacity the notorious Dr. Sacheverell passed through the town on his way to Salatin, to the living of which he was presented in May, 1711, though he had previously undergone a sentence of suspension from the performance of his clerical functions for preaching two sermons which the House of Commons regarded as "malicious, scandalous, and seditious libels." The populace espoused the cause of Sacheverell, and his journey was a continued "tour of triumph." In Bristol he was carried in a procession on men's shoulders, amidst the waving of flags, the display of handkerchiefs, and the shouts and huzzas of the assembled multitude. As the procession approached the building where Fleet was at work, he, in mere sport, hung a halter on a pole, and waved it from a window. This was considered a sign of contempt, and caused an attack on the house. Stones and other missiles were thrown at the windows, the doors were broken in, and search was made for the offender, who in the mean time, had gone to the top of the building, and passing from the roof of one house to another, at length descended into an unfrequented street, and made his escape. He went to London, and remained there for some time. After a while, supposing that his offence had been forgotten, he returned to Bristol, but found that he was watched, and likely to get into trouble. He thought it prudent, therefore, to put the ocean between himself and danger. He made his way to this country, and landed in Boston in 1712. Whether he brought any property with him is not known. But soon after his arrival he established a printing-house in Pudding Lane (now Devonshire Street), and carried on the printing of ballads, pamphlets, and small books for children. Being industrious and frugal, he gradually accumulated property. It was not long before he became acquainted with "the wealthy family of Goose," a branch of which he had before known in Bristol. The result we have already seen. The happy couple took up their residence in the same house with the printing-office in Pudding Lane. In due time, their family was increased by the birth of a son and heir. Like most mothers-in-law, Mrs. Goose found her importance increase with the appearance of her grandchild, and like all good grandmothers she was in ecstasies at the event. Following the example of her namesake, the celebrated "Goosey, goosey, gander," she spent her whole time in wandering about the house,—

"Up stairs, and down stairs,
And in my lady's chamber," —

taking care of the baby, and crooning to it the ditties she had learned in her younger days, until poor Mr. Fleet, half distracted with her endless strains, and finding that, as she was not to be put down, he must submit to the infliction, resolved to write down the songs the old lady was in the habit of singing, and to collect what more he could from other sources, and then to publish them for the benefit of the world — not forgetting himself. This he did, bringing forth a book which bore the following title : "Songs for the Nursery, or Mother Goose's Melodies for children. Printed by T. Fleet, at his printing-house, Pudding Lane, 1719. Price two coppers." Something probably intended to represent a goose with a very long neck and a mouth wide open, covered a large part of the page. The adoption of this title was very characteristic of Fleet, as he was never known to spare his nearest friends when he could excite laughter at their expense.

Three years after the death of her husband, and two years before the marriage of

Fleet to her daughter, "Mother Goose," as executrix of the estate of Isaac Vergoose with the advice and consent of the "overseers" of the will, mortgaged part of said estate to John Cutler of Boston, physician, for the sum of £150, from which it may be inferred that her income was not very large. This was on the 20th of August, 1713. The money was repaid, and the mortgage cancelled 1719-20. But the same year, the income, not being sufficient to meet the expenses of the family, she made sale, in accordance with the provisions of the will, of part of the estate to Jonathan Simpson of Boston, periwig maker, for the sum of " 400 pounds of good bills of credit of the province." In 1729, Peter, the youngest child, became of age, and the children by the second wife were at liberty, under the will, to divide their share of their father's property among themselves. The first step was to obtain a quitclaim deed from the widow, which they proceeded to do. It was as follows: "To all People to whom these Presents shall come Elizabeth Vergoose of Boston in the county of Suffolk and province of Massachusetts Bay in New England widow late the wife of Isaac Vergoose of Boston afores[d] Carter dec[d] sendeth Greeting Know ye that I the said Elizabeth Vergoose for and in consideration of the Sum of Five Shillings Money to me in hand . . . paid by Thomas Fleet Printer and Elizabeth his wife Anna Vergoose Spinster Isaac Vergoose Ship joyner Peter Vergoose Shipwright all of Boston afores[d] The Receipt whereof I do hereby acknowlledge as also for divers other causes & Considerations me thereunto moving I the s[d] Elizabeth Vergoose Have remised Released and . . Quit Claimed unto the said Thomas Fleet and Elizabeth his Wife Anna Vergoose Isaac Vergoose & Peter Vergoose All the Right Title Interest Claim and Demand whatsoever which I and my Heirs have or by any means may have of in & unto three certain Messuages or Dwelling Houses with the land whereon the same do stand and is thereunto belonging and whereof the said Isaac Vergoose Dec[d] dyed seized in Fee lying and being in Newbury Street so called in Boston afores[d]." The deed, from which this is an extract, is dated and was recorded May 27, 1735. With this document "Mother Goose" disappears from the stage, though she must have lived for more than twenty years afterward ; for, on the 25th of March, 1757, Ann Vergoose was appointed "administratrix on the goods and estate of her mother Elizabeth Vergoose lately deceased." Her age was 92 years or thereabouts. An inventory of her estate was ordered to be returned before the 24th day of March, 1758. The return was not made, however, until the 13th day of April, 1759. It was as follows : —

	£	s.	d.
1 Large square Looking Glass .	1	4	-
1 Small Looking Glass . . .		6	-
6 Turkey work'd Chairs at ¼		8	-
9 Green Chairs, & one old arm chair at 8d . .		6	8
5 Old Leather Chairs at 9d		3	9

	£	s.	d.
2 Joint Stools at 8ᵈ		1	4
28ᵇ Old Pewter at 10ᵈ	1	4	6
1 Old fashion Chest of Draws		5	4
1 Large Maple Table		8	–
1 Pʳ. Cover'd Brass handirons		5	–
1 Pʳ. Iron Dogs ⅟ 1 Iron Dog 4ᵈ		2	–
2 Spits 1 Pʳ. Tongs 1 Shovel & 1 Trammel		5	4
1 Iron pott 1 Skillett	1	6	–
30ᵇ Old Brass at 11ᵈ	1	7	6
1 Old Trunk 12ᵈ 1 Stone Jug ⅟		3	–
1 Pʳ. Sheets, ⅟ 1 Table Cloth ⅟ 2 pillow cases ⅟		16	8
1 Large Silver Tankard, wᵗ 42 ounces, at ⅟	13	9	6
1 Silver bason 1 Cup & 4 old Spoons wᵗ 19ᵒˢ 9ᵈʷᵗ	6	4	⅟
Whole Amount,	£27	2	1¾

Six months afterward, or on the 24th of November, 1759, Ann brought in an account against the old lady which swallowed up not only all that was left, according to the Inventory, but upwards of £40 more. The following is a copy of it : —

Dr Estate of Elizᵗ Vergoose decᵈ with Anna Vergoose

		£	s.	d.
1754	Administrator			
March 17ᵗʰ To Meat Drink Washing & lodging &c for 14 years 9 moᵗʰˢ:				
& 20 days at £6 : 13 : 4. ⅌ Year		98	11 : 9	
To 4 Years ditto when Lame &c.		53	6 : 8	
To Cash paid for Medicines		2	9 : 8	
To Funeral Charges		3	–	–
		157	8 : 1	
To Letters of Administration &c			10 : –	
To Exhibiting the Inventory Oaths &c			2 : 6	
To Examining allowing and Recording this Accᵒ			5 : –	
		£158	5 : 7	

1754
March 17ᵗʰ   Cᵗ ———

	£	s.	d.
By Isaac Vergoose's Bond not paid,	£31	6 .	10
By Thoˢ. Fleet's Bond balᶜᵉ. due	20	1 :	1½
By my own Bond,	31 ·	6 :	10

By Peter Vergoose Bond to his decease	.	7 : 10 : —
By Goods as ♥ Apprisement . .	. .	27 : 2 : 1¼

£117 : 6 : 10¾

Errors Excepted

ANNA VERGOOSE

One cannot take leave of " Mother Goose " without a benediction upon her memory ; for to her we are all — we of America, at least — under obligations which we may gratefully acknowledge, but can never adequately discharge. Was it not she who soothed us to sleep with her simple lullabies in our hours of infancy, and who, in our childhood, "oped the fount of sympathetic tears " by her tragic tales, or evoked " sincerest laughter," unfraught with pain, by her comicalities, or held us spell-bound by her marvellous stories, which not even the audacious Munchausen himself, in the boldest flights of his imagination, ever equalled ? And though we must admit that her taste might sometimes have been more refined, and that her morality was not always of the purest, shall we, to whom her worst descriptions of theft and murder and barbarity were either " full of sound and fury, signifying nothing " or at least were unaccompanied by a realizing sense of the "ghastly horror " or of the " gross vulgarity " which has been charged upon them, — shall we listen with any patience to those who malign her as " A Witch in the Nursery "? *
" Truth is," said Sir Walter Scott, " I would not give one tear shed over Little Red Riding Hood for all the benefit to be derived from a hundred histories of Jemmy Goodchild. I think the selfish tendencies will be soon enough acquired in this arithmetical age ; and that, to make the higher class of character, our own wild fictions — like our own simple music, — will have more effect in awakening the fancy and elevating the disposition than the colder and more elaborate compositions of modern authors and composers." It is not to be pretended that Mother Goose will help " to make the higher class of character," or that she will do much towards " elevating the disposition," but that her melodies are all of them harmless, and many of them charming, and that they do tend to " awaken the fancy," and stimulate the imagination, and nourish a sense of the humorous, may safely be asserted. Those who prefer morality combined with inanity or insipidity, can find enough of it in many of the juvenile works of our day.

To come back to our history. Thomas Fleet in 1731 rented a new brick building at the corner of Cornhill (now the lower part of Washington Street) and Water Street, which he afterwards purchased, and in which he spent the remainder of his days. The house was spacious, and afforded rooms for the accommodation of his family, and for the transaction of his business. To his occupation as a printer and

* See an article with this title in *Household Words*, vol. iii., No. 78.

b

bookseller, he added that of an auctioneer. In the "Boston News Letter" of March 7, 1731, he describes his place of business as in "Cornhill at the Sign of the Heart and Crown, near the lower end of School Street," and gives notice that he has a "large and commodious front room fit for *this business*, and a *Talent* well known and approved." In the same year he was employed to print the fifth newspaper which was published in Boston. This was the "Weekly Rehearsal," the first number of which was issued September 27, 1731. Jeremiah Gridley was the "author," or editor. In 1733, Fleet, who had for some time been interested in the publication, became the sole proprietor. He continued the publication under the same name until August 21, 1735, when the title was changed to "The Boston Evening Post." The "Post" soon became the most popular of the Boston newspapers. It often contained specimens of the wit and drollery for which Fleet was noted, as witness the following advertisement: "To be sold, by the printer of this paper, the very best negro woman in town, who has had the small-pox and the measles ; is as hearty as a horse, as brisk as a bird, will work like a beaver." Having occasion to complain of delinquent subscribers, among whom were some of great religious pretensions, he said in an editorial paragraph, "Every one thinks he has a right to read news, but few find themselves inclined to pay for it. 'Tis a great pity a soil that will bear *piety* so well, should not produce a tolerable crop of *honesty*."

It is traditionally reported that Fleet was not blessed with as sweet-tempered a wife and daughters as he could have wished for. On one occasion he invited a friend to dine with him on *pouts*, a kind of fish then esteemed a great delicacy, and of which he knew his friend to be remarkably fond. His domestic affairs, however, did not move along very smoothly that day, and when they sat down to table the gentleman remarked that the *pouts* were wanting. "Oh, no," said Fleet, "only look at my wife and daughters !"

Thomas Fleet died July 21, 1758, aged nearly 73 years. The publication of the "Evening Post" was continued by his sons, Thomas and John, until April 17, 1775, when it was discontinued, having been in existence under the Fleets upwards of forty years. The inventory of Fleet's estate was presented at the Probate Office in January, 1759. The whole amount was £959 2s. 2d.

Elizabeth Fleet survived her husband for seventeen years, dying in 1775, at the age of 81. From all accounts she was a singular character, and inherited much of her father's disposition, acting upon the principle of "Keep what you've got, and get what you can." She retained possession almost as long as she lived of the lot that was set off to her after her father's death. The income from it, and from all the other property which came to her from her father's estate, she kept in her own hands. This must have amounted to a considerable sum. The Cornhill house, spoken of above, which was bought of James Bowdoin, in 1744, for £650, is said to have been paid for with her money, the savings from her income. She had seven children, four

sons and three daughters. The first two, a son and a daughter, died young ; the
others survived her. John Fleet, the youngest child, was born September 25, 1734,
and died March 18, 1806. He married Elizabeth Cazneau, and had five children
by her, of whom the youngest, Ann, died July 30, 1860, at the age of 89 years, being
the last of the family that bore the name of Fleet.

Isaac Goose, the brother of Mrs. Fleet, and the oldest son of " Mother Goose,"
was a ship-joiner. He married, in 1734 or earlier, somebody named Elizabeth, of
Stoughton, by whom he had several children. The last of these, a daughter, died
in June, 1807, and with her the name, but not the fame, of Goose became extinct.

"PEOPLE may talk of Homer and Shakespeare, and whom they please of that class, but Mother Goose may hold up her head with the best of them. The Swan of Avon is not the only bird that has made melody for all time. See how Mother Goose has stood her ground, and survived whole generations and ages of pretenders to poetical inspiration. How many great writers have sprung up from nothing, flourished away, and sunk back to nothing, while Mother Goose has sat calmly brooding over her golden eggs of wisdom! What revolutions and overturns we have had in literature, to the utter demolition of great names and great reputations in poetry! What fluctuations between the lake school, the metaphysical school, the romantic school, the transcendental school, the namby-pamby school, and the fiddle-de-dee school, sending thousands of sprouting and aspiring poets into everlasting oblivion! Amidst all these tossings and turnings, and ups and downs of popular opinion, Mother Goose has swum like a duck, and kept her glorious reputation above water."

LIST OF ILLUSTRATIONS.

MOTHER GOOSE'S MELODIES.

A, B, C, and D,
Pray, playmates, agree.
E, F, and G,
Well, so it shall be.
J, K, and L,
In peace we will dwell.
M, N, and O,
To play let us go.
P, Q, R, and S,
Love may we possess.
W, X, and Y,
Will not quarrel or die.
Z and amperse-and,
Go to school at command.

A cat came fiddling out of a barn,
With a pair of bag-pipes under her arm;
She could sing nothing but fiddle de dee,
The mouse has married the humble-bee;
Pipe, cat, — dance, mouse, —
We'll have a wedding at our good house.

ı

A, B, C, tumble down D,
The cat's in the cupboard, and can't see me.

———+———

About the bush, Willy,
 About the bee-hive,
About the bush, Willy,
 I'll meet thee alive.
Then to my ten shillings
 Add you but a groat,
I'll go to Newcastle,
 And buy a new coat.
Five and five shillings,
 Five and a crown;
Five and five shillings
 Will buy a new gown.
Five and five shillings,
 Five and a groat;
Five and five shillings
 Will buy a new coat.

———+———

A carrion crow sat on an oak,[1]
Fol de riddle, lol de riddle, hi ding do,
Watching a tailor shape his cloak;
Sing heigh ho, the carrion crow,
Fol de riddle, lol de riddle, hi ding do.

Wife, bring me my old bent bow,
Fol de riddle, lol de riddle, hi ding do,

That I may shoot yon carrion crow;
Sing heigh ho, the carrion crow,
Fol de riddle, lol de riddle, hi ding do.

The tailor he shot, and missed his mark,
Fol de riddle, lol de riddle, hi ding do,
And shot his own sow quite through the heart;
Sing heigh ho, the carrion crow,
Fol de riddle, lol de riddle, hi ding do.

Wife, bring brandy in a spoon,
Fol de riddle, lol de riddle, hi ding do,
For our old sow is in a swoon;
Sing heigh ho, the carrion crow,
Fol de riddle, lol de riddle, hi ding do.

———•———

A cow and a calf,
An ox and a half,
Forty good shillings and three;
Is that not enough tocher[2]
For a shoemaker's daughter,
A bonny lass with a black e'e?

———•———

A cow and a calf,
An ox and a half,
A church and a steeple,
And all the good people,
And yet he complained that his stomach wasn't full.

A dillar, a dollar,
A ten o'clock scholar,
What makes you come so soon?
You used to come at ten o'clock,
And now you come at noon.

———•———

A dog and a cat went out together,   .
To see some friends just out of town;
  Said the cat to the dog,
" What d'ye think of the weather?"
" I think, ma'am, the rain will come down;
But don't be alarmed, for I 've an umbrella
That will shelter us both," said this amiable fellow.

———•———

A dog and a cock
A journey once took,
They travelled along till 'twas late;
  The dog he made free
  In the hollow of a tree
And the cock on the boughs of it sate.

The cock, nothing knowing,
In the morn fell a-crowing,
Upon which comes a fox to the tree;
  Says he, "I declare,
  Your voice is above
All the creatures I ever did see.

" O ! would you come down,
I a favorite might own."
Said the cock, " There's a porter below ;
If you will go in,
I promise I'll come down."
So he went — and was worried for it, too.

———

A duck and a drake,[3]
A nice barley-cake,
With a penny to pay the old baker ;
A hop and a scotch
Is another notch,
Slitherum, slatherum, take her.

———

A for the Ape, that we saw at the fair ;
B for a Blockhead, who ne'er shall go there ;
C for a Cauliflower, white as a curd ;
D for a Duck, a very good bird ;
E for an Egg, good in pudding or pies ;
F for a Farmer, rich, honest, and wise ;
G for a Gentleman, void of all care ;
H for the Hound, that ran down the hare ;
I for an Indian, sooty and dark ;
K for the Keeper, that looked to the park ;
L for a Lark, that soared in the air ;
M for a Mole, that ne'er could get there ;
N for Sir Nobody, ever in fault ;
O for an Otter, that ne'er could be caught ;

P for a Pudding, stuck full of plums ;
Q was for Quartering it, see here he comes ;
R for a Rook, that croaked in the trees ;
S for a Sailor, that ploughed the deep seas ;
T for a Top, that doth prettily spin ;
V for a Virgin of delicate mien ;
W for Wealth, in gold, silver, and pence ;
X for old Xenophon, noted for sense ;
Y for a Yew, which for ever is green ;   .
Z for the Zebra, that belongs to the queen.

A horse and cart
Had Billy Smart,
To play when it pleased him ;
The cart he'd load
By the side of the road,
And be happy if no one teased him.

A little boy went into a barn,
And lay down on some hay ;
An owl came out and flew about,
And the little boy ran away.

A little cock-sparrow sat on a tree,
Looking as happy as happy could be,
Till a boy came by, with his bow and arrow :
Says he, " I will shoot the little cock-sparrow.

Mother Goose's Melodies.

"His body will make me a nice little stew,
And his giblets will make me a little pie, too."
Says the little cock-sparrow, "I'll be shot if I stay,"
So he clapped his wings, and flew away.

———•———

As I was going to St. Ives,
I met a man with seven wives,
Every wife had seven sacks,
Every sack had seven cats,
Every cat had seven kits :
Kits, cats, sacks, and wives,
How many were there going to St. Ives?

———•———

A frog he would a-wooing go,
     Sing, heigho, says Rowley,
Whether his mother would let him or no ;
With a rowley, powley, gammon, and spinach,
     Heigho, says Anthony Rowley.

So off he marched with his opera hat,
     Heigho, says Rowley.
And on the way he met with a rat,
     With a rowley, powley, etc.

And when they came to mouse's hall,
     Heigho, says Rowley,
They gave a loud knock, and they gave a loud call,
     With a rowley, powley, etc.

Mother Goose's Melodies.

" Pray, Mrs. Mouse, are you within ? "
    Heigho, says Rowley ;
" Yes, kind sir, I am sitting to spin,"
    With a rowley, powley, etc.

" Pray, Mrs. Mouse, will you give us some beer ? "
    Heigho, says Rowley;
" For Froggy and I are fond of good cheer,"
    With a rowley, powley, etc.

Now while they all were a merry-making,
    Heigho, says Rowley,
The cat and her kittens came tumbling in,
    With a rowley, powley, etc.

The cat she seized the rat by the crown,
    Heigho, says Rowley,
The kittens they pulled the little mouse down,
    With a rowley, powley, etc.

This put poor frog in a terrible fright,
    Heigho, says Rowley,
So he took up his hat and wished them good-night,
    With a rowley, powley, etc.

But as Froggy was crossing over a brook,
    Heigho, says Rowley,
A lily-white duck came and gobbled him up,
    With a rowley, powley, etc.

So there was an end of one, two, and three,
    Heigho, says Rowley,
The rat, the mouse, and the little Frog-ee!
With a rowley, powley, gammon, and spinach,
    Heigho, says Anthony Rowley.

A little old man and I fell out;
How shall we bring this matter about?
Bring it about as well you can,
Get you gone, you little old man!

A little old man of Derby,
How do you think he served me?
He took away my bread and cheese,
And that is how he served me.

A little pig found a fifty-dollar note,
And purchased a hat and a very fine coat,
  With trousers, and stockings, and shoes;
Cravat, and shirt-collar, and gold-headed cane;
Then proud as could be, did he march up the lane,
  Says he, "I shall hear all the news."

A long-tailed pig, or a short-tailed pig,
  Or a pig without e'er a tail,
A sow-pig, or a boar-pig,
  Or a pig with a curly tail.

A-milking, a-milking, my maid,
" Cow, take care of your heels," she said ;
" And you shall have some nice new hay,
If you'll quietly let me milk away."

An old woman was sweeping her house, and she found
a little crooked sixpence.   "What," said she, "shall I do
with this little sixpence?   I will go to market, and buy a
little pig."   As she was coming home, she came to a stile :
the piggy would not go over the stile.

She went a little further, and she met a dog. So she
said to the dog, " Dog! bite pig ; piggy won't go over the
stile ; and I shan't get home to-night."   But the dog would
not.

She went a little further, and she met a stick. So she
said, " Stick ! stick ! beat dog ; dog won't bite pig ; piggy
won't get over the stile ; and I shan't get home to-night."
But the stick would not.

She went a little further, and she met a fire. So she
said, " Fire ! fire ! burn stick ; stick won't beat dog ; dog
won't bite pig " [and so forth, always repeating the fore-
going words].   But the fire would not.

She went a little further, and she met some water. So
she said, " Water ! water ! quench fire ; fire won't burn
stick," etc.   But the water would not.

She went a little further, and she met an ox. So she
said, " Ox ! ox ! drink water ; water won't quench fire," etc.
But the ox would not.

She went a little further, and she met a butcher. So

she said, " Butcher! butcher! kill ox; ox won't drink water,"
etc. But the butcher would not.

She went a little further, and she met a rope. So she
said, "Rope! rope! hang butcher; butcher won't kill ox,"
etc. But the rope would not.

She went a little further, and she met a rat. So she
said, " Rat! rat! gnaw rope; rope won't hang butcher," etc.
But the rat would not.

She went a little further, and she met a cat. So she
said, "Cat! cat! kill rat; rat won't gnaw rope," etc. But
the cat said to her, "If you will go to yonder cow, and
fetch me a saucer of milk, I will kill the rat." So away
went the old woman to the cow.

But the cow said to her, "If you will go to yonder hay-
stack, and fetch me a handful of hay, I'll give you the
milk." So away went the old woman to the haystack ; and
she brought the hay to the cow.

As soon as the cow had eaten the hay, she gave the
old woman the milk ; so away she went with it in a saucer
to the cat.

As soon as the cat had lapped up the milk, the cat
began to kill the rat; the rat began to gnaw the rope; the
rope began to hang the butcher; the butcher began to kill
the ox ; the ox began to drink the water ; the water began
to quench the fire ; the fire began to burn the stick ; the
stick began to beat the dog ; the dog began to bite the pig ;
the little pig in a fright jumped over the stile ; and so the
old woman got home that night.

A man of words and not of deeds[4]
Is like a garden full of weeds ;
For when the weeds begin to grow,
Then doth the garden overflow.

———•———

Apple-pie, pudding, and pancake,
All begins with A.

———•———

A riddle, a riddle, as I suppose,[5]
A hundred eyes, and never a nose.

———•———

Arthur O'Bower has broken his band,[6]
He comes roaring up the land ; —
The King of Scots, with all his power,
Cannot turn Arthur of the Bower!

———•———

As I walked by myself,[7]
And talked to myself,
Myself said unto me,
Look to thyself,
Take care of thyself,
For nobody cares for thee.

I answered myself,
And said to myself
In the self-same repartee,

Look to thyself
Or not look to thyself,
The self-same thing will be.

———•———

As I was going up Pippen Hill, —
Pippen Hill was dirty, —
There I met a pretty miss,
And she dropped me a curtsey.

Little miss, pretty miss,
Blessings light upon you!
If I had half-a-crown a day,
I'd spend it all upon you.

———•———

As I was going along, long, long,
A-singing a comical song, song, song,
The lane that I went was so long, long, long,
And the song that I sung was as long, long, long,
And so I went singing along.

———•———

As I was going o'er London Bridge,[8]
I met a cart full of fingers and thumbs!

———•———

As I was going o'er London Bridge,[9]
And peeped through a nick,
I saw four and twenty ladies
Riding on a stick!

As I was going o'er Tipple Tine,[10]
I met a flock of bonny swine;
    Some green-lapped,
    Some green-backed :
They were the very bonniest swine
That e'er went over Tipple Tine.

As I was going o'er Westminster Bridge,
I met with a Westminster scholar ;
He pulled off his cap *an' drew* off his glove,
And wished me a very good morrow.
    What is his name ?

As I was going to sell my eggs,
I met a man with bandy legs,
Bandy legs and crooked toes,
I tripped up his heels, and he fell on his nose.

    As I was going up the hill,
      I met with Jack the piper,
    And all the tune that he could play
      Was, "Tie up your petticoats tighter."

    I tied them once, I tied them twice,
      I tied them three times over ;
    And all the song that he could sing
      Was, "Carry me safe to Dover."

As I was walking o'er little Moorfields,
I saw St. Paul's a-running on wheels,
 With a fee, fo, fum.
Then for further frolics I'll go to France,
While Jack shall sing and his wife shall dance,
 With a fee, fo, fum.

———•———

 As I went over the water,
  The water went over me.
 I saw two little blackbirds
  Sitting on a tree.
 The one called me a rascal,
  The other called me a thief ;
 I took up my little black stick,
  And knocked out all their teeth.

———•———

As I went through the garden gap,[11]
Who should I meet but Dick Red-cap !
A stick in his hand, a stone in his throat.
If you'll tell me this riddle, I'll give you a groat.

———•———

 As I went to Bonner,
  I met a pig
  Without a wig.
 Upon my word and nonor.

As round as an apple, as deep as a cup,[12]
And all the king's horses can't pull it up.

As soft as silk, as white as milk,[13]
As bitter as gall, a thick wall,
And a green coat covers me all.

When the days begin to lengthen,
The cold begins to strengthen.

As titty-mouse sat in the witty to spin,[14]
Pussy came to her and bid her good e'en,
" O what are you doing, my little 'oman?"
" A-spinning a doublet for my gude man."
" Then shall I come to thee and wind up thy thread?"
" O no, Mrs. Puss, you will bite off my head."

As Tommy Snooks and Bessy Brooks
Were walking out one Sunday,
Says Tommy Snooks to Bessy Brooks,
" To-morrow will be Monday."

A sunshiny shower
Won't last half an hour.

A swarm of bees in May
Is worth a load of hay ;
A swarm of bees in June
Is worth a silver spoon ;
A swarm of bees in July
Is not worth a fly.

At Dover Dwells George Brown Esquire,[15]
Good Christopher Finch, And David Friar.

A thatcher of Thatchwood went to Thatchet a-thatching
Did a thatcher of Thatchwood go to Thatchet a-thatching ?
If a thatcher of Thatchwood went to Thatchet a-thatching,
Where's the thatching the thatcher of Thatchwood has
    thatched ?

At the battle of the Nile,
I was there all the while,
All the while, all the while,
At the battle of the Nile.

Awa', birds, away ![16]
Take a little, leave a little,
And do not come again ;
For if you do,
I will shoot you through,
And there is an end of you.

2

Awake, arise, pull out your eyes,
  And hear what time of day;
And when you have done, pull out your tongue,
  And see what you can say.

———•———

A was an apple-pie;[17]
B bit it;
C cut it;
D dealt it;
E eat it;
F fought for it;
G got it;
H had it;
J joined it;
K kept it;
L longed for it;
M mourned for it;
N nodded at it;
O opened it;
P peeped in it;
Q quartered it;
R ran for it;
S stole it;
T took it;
V viewed it;
W wanted it;
X, Y, Z, and amperse-and,
All wished for a piece in hand.

Bobby Shafto 's gone to sea,[18]
With silver buckles at his knee;
When he comes back he'll marry me, —
  Pretty Bobby Shafto!

Bobby Shafto 's fat and fair,
Combing down his yellow hair,
He's my love for evermore, —
  Pretty Bobby Shafto!

———

A was an Archer, and shot at a frog;[19]
B was a Butcher, and had a great dog.
C was a Captain, all covered with lace;
D was a Drunkard, and had a red face.
E was an Esquire, with pride on his brow;
F was a Farmer, and followed the plough.
G was a Gamester, who had but ill·luck;
H was a Hunter, and hunted a buck.
I was an Inn-keeper, who loved to bouse;[20]
J was a Joiner, and built up a house.
K was King William, once governed this land:
L was a Lady, who had a white hand.
M was a Miser, and hoarded up gold;
N was a Nobleman, gallant and bold.
O was an Oyster-wench, and went about town,
P was a Parson, and wore a black gown.
Q was a Queen, who was fond of good flip:
R was a Robber, and wanted a whip.

S was a Sailor, and spent all he got ;
T was a Tinker, and mended a pot.
U was a Usurer, a miserable elf ;
V was a Vintner, who drank all himself.
W was a Watchman, and guarded the door ;
X was eXpensive, and so became poor.
Y was a Youth, that did not love school ;
Z was a Zany, a poor, harmless fool.

———•———

Baa, baa, black sheep,
  Have you any wool ?
Yes, marry,[21] have I,
  Three bags full ;
One for my master,
  And one for my dame,
But none for the little boy
  Who cries in the lane.

———•———

Barnaby Bright he was a sharp cur,[22]
He always would bark if a mouse did but stir ;
But now he's grown old, and no longer can bark,
He's condemned by the parson to be hanged by the clerk.[23]

———•———

Bell-horses, bell-horses,
  What time of day ?
One o'clock, two o'clock,
  Off and away.

Bessy Bell and Mary Gray,[24]
　They were two bonny lasses ;
They built their house upon the lea,
　And covered it with rashes.

Bessy kept the garden gate,
　And Mary kept the pantry ;
Bessy always had to wait,
　While Mary lived in plenty.

———·———

Birds of a feather flock together,
　And so will pigs and swine ;
Rats and mice will have their choice,
　And so will I have mine.

———·———

Black within, and red without ;[25]
Four corners round about.

———·———

Black we are, but much admired ;[26]
Men seek for us till they are tired ;
We tire the horse, but comfort man ;
Tell me this riddle if you can.

———·———

Bless you, bless you, burnie bee ;[27]
Say, when will your wedding be ?
If it be to-morrow day,
Take your wings and fly away.

Blue eye beauty,
Grey eye greedy,
Black eye blackie,
Brown eye brownie.

———————

Bounce buckram, velvet's dear ;
Christmas comes but once a year.

———————

Bow, wow, wow,
Whose dog art thou ?
Little Tom Tinker's dog,
Bow, wow, wow.

———————

Buff says Buff to all his men,[28]
And I say Buff to you again ;
Buff neither laughs nor smiles,
But carries his face
With a very good grace,
And passes the stick to the very next place !

———————

Bryan O'Lin, and his wife, and wife's mother,[29]
They all went over the bridge together ;
The bridge was broken, and they all fell in,
The deuce go with all ! quoth Bryan O'Lin.

Buz, quoth the blue fly,[30]
Hum, quoth the bee;
Buz and hum, they cry,
And so do we.
In his ear, in his nose,
Thus, do you see?
He ate the dormouse,
Else it was he.

———•———

Bye, baby bumpkin,
Where's Tony Lumpkin?
My lady 's on her death-bed,
With eating half a pumpkin.

———•———

Bye, baby bunting,[30a]
Daddy's gone a hunting,
To get a little rabbit's skin
To wrap the baby bunting in.

———•———

Catch him, crow! carry him, kite!
Take him away till the apples are ripe;
When they are ripe and ready to fall,
Home comes [*Johnny*], apples and all.

———•———

Charley loves good cake and ale,
Charley loves good candy,

Charley loves to kiss the girls,
  When they are clean and handy.

———

Cock a doodle doo!
My dame has lost her shoe;
My master's lost his fiddling-stick,
And don't know what to do.

Cock a doodle doo!
What is my dame to do?
Till master finds his fiddling-stick,
She'll dance without her shoe.

Cock a doodle doo!
My dame has lost her shoe,
And master's found his fiddling-stick.
Sing doodle doodle doo!

Cock a doodle doo!
My dame will dance with you,
While master fiddles his fiddling-stick,
For dame and doodle doo.

Cock a doodle doo!
Dame has lost her shoe;
Gone to bed and scratched her head,
And can't tell what to do.

TOM
TOM
THE
PIPER'S
SON
STOLE
A
PIG
AND
AWAY
HE
RUN.
—

Hey ! diddle, diddle,[31]
The cat and the fiddle,
The cow jumped over the moon ;
The little dog laughed
To see such sport,
And the dish ran away with the spoon.

Cock Robin got up early,
At the break of day,
And went to Jenny's window,
To sing a roundelay.

He sang Cock Robin's love
To the pretty Jenny Wren,
And when he got unto the end,
Then he began again.

Cold and raw the north winds blow,
Bleak in the morning early ;
All the hills are covered with snow,
And winter's now come fairly.

Come, butter, come,[32]
Come, butter, come !
Peter stands at the gate,
Waiting for a buttered cake ;
Come, butter, come !

Come, dance a jig
To my granny's pig,
With a raudy, rowdy, dowdy;
Come, dance a jig
To my granny's pig,
And pussy-cat shall crowdy.[83]

———

Come listen, my boys, sit still and be mum,
I'll read the apparel of Master Tom Thumb.
An oaken leaf he had for his crown;
His shirt it was by spiders spun;
His stockings of thistle-down, they tie
With eyelash picked from his mother's eye;
His hat was made of butterfly's wing;
His boots were wove of gossamer thin;
His coat and breeches were shaped with pride;
A needle mounted swung by his side;
A mouse he rode as his dapple steed;
His bridle curb an inch of thread;
His shoes were made of a squirrel's skin,
Nicely tanned, the hair within.

———

Come when you're called,
Do what you're bid,
Shut the door after you,
Never be chid.

"Croak !" said the toad, " I'm hungry, I think ;
To-day I've had nothing to eat or to drink.
I'll crawl to a garden and jump through the pales,
And there I'll dine nicely on slugs and on snails."
" Ho, ho !" quoth the frog, " is that what you mean ?
Then I'll hop away to the next meadow stream ;
There I will drink, and eat worms and slugs too,
And then I shall have a good dinner like you."

Cross patch,
Draw the latch,
Sit by the fire and spin ;
Take a cup,
And drink it up,
Then call your neighbors in.

Curly locks ! curly locks ! wilt thou be mine ?
Thou shalt not wash dishes, nor yet feed the swine ;
But sit on a cushion and sew a fine seam,
And feed upon strawberries, sugar, and cream !

Cushy cow bonny, let down thy milk,
And I will give thee a gown of silk ;
A gown of silk and a silver tee,[34]
If thou wilt let down thy milk to me.

Dame, get up and bake your pies,
Bake your pies, bake your pies ;
Dame, get up and bake your pies,
On Christmas-day in the morning.

Dame, what makes your maidens lie,
Maidens lie, maidens lie ;
Dame, what makes your maidens lie,
On Christmas-day in the morning ?

Dame, what makes your ducks to die,
Ducks to die, ducks to die ;
Dame, what makes your ducks to die,
On Christmas-day in the morning ?

Their wings are cut, and they cannot fly,
Cannot fly, cannot fly ;
Their wings are cut, and they cannot fly,
On Christmas-day in the morning.

———•———

Dance, little baby, dance up high,
Never mind, baby, mother is by ;
Crow and caper, caper and crow,
There, little baby, there you go ;
Up to the ceiling, down to the ground,
Backwards and forwards, round and round ;
Dance, little baby, and mother will sing,
With the merry coral, ding, ding, ding !

Dance, Thumbkin, dance,
[*Keep the thumb in motion.*]

Dance, ye merry men, every one:
[*All the fingers in motion.*]

For Thumbkin he can dance alone,
[*The thumb only moving.*]

Thumbkin he can dance alone,
[*The thumb only moving.*]

Dance, Foreman, dance,
[*The first finger moving.*]

Dance, ye merry men, every one:
[*The whole moving.*]

But Foreman he can dance alone,
Foreman he can dance alone.
[*The first finger only moving.*]

Dance, Longman, dance,
[*The second finger only moving.*]

Dance, ye merry men, every one:
[*The whole moving.*]

But Longman he can dance alone,
Longman he can dance alone.
[*And so on with the others, naming the third finger* Ringman, *and the fourth finger* Littleman. *Littleman cannot dance alone.*]

Dance to your daddy,
My little babby;
Dance to your daddy,
My little lamb.

You shall have a fishy,
In a little dishy;
You shall have a fishy
When the boat comes in.

———•———

Danty baby diddy,
What can a mammy do wid'e,
But sit in a lap,
And give 'un a pap?
Sing danty baby diddy.

———•———

Dear Sensibility, O la!
I heard a little lamb cry, baa!
Says I, "So you have lost mamma?"
                              " Baa !"

The little lamb, as I said so,
Frisking about the fields did go,
And, frisking, trod upon my toe.
                              " Oh !"

Pussy sits beside the fire,
    How can she be fair?
In comes the little dog,
    " Pussy, are you there?
So, so, dear Mistress Pussy,
    Pray tell me how do you do? "
" Thank you, thank you, little dog,
    I'm very well just now."

———

Deedle, deedle dumpling, my son John,
He went to bed with his stockings on ;
One stocking off, and one stocking on,
Deedle, deedle, dumpling, my son John.

———

Dickery, dickery, dare,
The pig flew up in the air ;
The man in brown soon brought him down,
Dickery, dickery, dare.

———

Diddledy, diddledy, dumpty ;
The cat ran up the plum-tree.
    I'll lay you a crown
    I'll fetch you down ;
So diddledy, diddledy, dumpty.

Did you see my wife, did you see, did you see,
Did you see my wife looking for me?
She wears a straw bonnet, with white ribbons on it,
And dimity petticoats over her knee.

Ding dong bell,
Pussy's in the well!
Who put her in? —
Little Johnny Green.
Who pulled her out? —
Big Johnny Stout.
What a naughty boy was that
To drown poor pussy cat,
Who never did him any harm,
But killed the mice in his father's barn!

Ding, dong, darrow;
The cat and the sparrow;
The little dog has burnt his tail,
And he shall be hanged to-morrow.

Dingty, diddlety, my mammy's maid,
She stole oranges, I am afraid;
Some in her pocket, some in her sleeve,
She stole oranges, I do believe.

Doctor Faustus was a good man,
He whipped his scholars now and then ;
When he whipped them, he made them dance
Out of Scotland into France,
Out of France into Spain,
And then he whipped them back again !

———+———

Doctor Foster went to Gloucester,
  In a shower of rain ;
He stepped into a puddle up to his middle,
  And never went there again.

———+———

Dogs in the garden, catch 'em, Towser ;
  Cows in the cornfield, run, boys, run ;
Cats in the cream-pot, run, girls, run, girls ;
  Fire on the mountains, run, boys, run.

———+———

Doodle, doodle, doo,
The princess lost her shoe ;
  Her highness hopped,
  The fiddler stopped,
Not knowing what to do.

———+———

Doodledy, doodledy, doodledy, dan,
I'll have a piper to be my good man ;
And if I get less meat, I shall get game,
Doodledy, doodledy, doodledy, dan.

Eggs, butter, bread,[35]
Stick, stock, stone dead !
Stick him up, stick him down,
Stick him in the old man's crown !

Elizabeth,. Elspeth, Betsy, and Bess,[36]
They all went together to seek a bird's nest.
They found a bird's nest with five eggs in,
They all took one, and left four in.

Every lady in this land[37]
Has twenty nails upon each hand
Five and twenty on hands and feet.
All this is true without deceit.

Eye winker,[38]
Tom tinker,
    Nose dropper,
Mouth eater,
 Chin chopper,
    Chin chopper.

Fa, Fe, Fi, Fo, Fum !
I smell the blood of an Englishman :
Be he alive or be he dead,
I'll grind his bones to make me bread

F for fig, J for jig,[39]
And N for knuckle bones,
I for Iohn the waterman,
And S for sack of stones.

———•———

Father Short came down the lane,
O! I'm obliged to hammer and smite
From four in the morning till eight at night,
For a bad master, and a worse dame.

———•———

Father Iohnson Nicholas Iohnson's son;
Son Iohnson Nicholas Iohnson's father.[40]

———•———

Fiddle-de-dee, fiddle-de-dee,
The fly shall marry the humble-bee.
They went to the church, and married was she,
The fly has married the humble-bee.

———•———

Flour of England, fruit of Spain,[41]
Met together in a shower of rain;
Put in a bag tied round with a string,
If you'll tell me this riddle, I'll give you a ring.

Gay go up, and gay go down,[42]
To ring the bells of London town.

Bull's eyes and targets,
Say the bells of St. Marg'ret's.

Brickbats and tiles,
Say the bells of St. Giles'.

Half-pence and farthings,
Say the bells of St. Martin's.

Oranges and lemons,
Say the bells of St. Clement's.

Pancakes and fritters,
Say the bells of St. Peter's.

Two sticks and an apple,
Say the bells at Whitechapel.

Old Father Baldpate,
Say the slow bells at Aldgate.

Pokers and tongs,
Say the bells at St. John's.

Kettles and pans,
Say the bells at St. Ann's.

You owe me ten shillings,
Say the bells at St. Helen's.

When will you pay me?
Say the bells at Old Bailey.

When I grow rich,
Say the bells at Shoreditch.

Pray, when will that be?
Say the bells of Stepney.

I am sure I don't know,
Says the great bell at Bow.

Here comes a candle to light you to bed,
And here comes a chopper to chop off your head.

———

Rowsty dowt, my fire 's all out,
My little dame is not at home?
I'll saddle my cock, and bridle my hen,
And fetch my little dame home again!
Home she came, tritty trot,
And asked for the porridge she left in the pot.
Some she ate, and some she shod,[43]
And some she gave to the truckler's dog;
She took up the ladle and knocked its head,
And now poor Dapsy dog is dead.

Four and twenty tailors went to kill a snail,
The best man among them durst not touch her tail ;
She put out her horns like a little Kyloe cow,
Run, tailors, run, or she'll kill you all e'en now.

———

Gilly Silly Jarter,
Who has lost a garter?
In a shower of rain,
The miller found it,
The miller ground it,
And the miller gave it to Silly again.

———

Girls and boys, come out to play,[43a]
The moon doth shine as bright as day ;
Leave your supper, and leave your sleep,
And come with your playfellows into the street.
Come with a whoop, come with a call,
Come with a good will or not at all.
Up the ladder and down the wall,
A half-penny roll will serve us all.
You find milk, and I'll find flour,
And we'll have a pudding in half an hour.

———

Give me a blow, and I'll beat 'em,
Why did they vex my baby ?
Kissy, kiss, kissy, my honey,
And cuddle your nurse, my deary.

Good Queen Bess was a glorious dame,
When bonny King Jemmy from Scotland came ;
    We'll pepper their bodies,
    Their peaceable noddies,
And give them a crack of the crown !

    Goosey, goosey, gander,
    Who stands yonder ?
    Little Betsey Baker ;
    Take her up, and shake her.

    Goosey, goosey, gander,
    Where shall I wander ?
    Up stairs, down stairs,
    And in my lady's chamber ;

    There I met an old man
    That would not say his prayers ;
    I took him by the left leg,
    And threw him down stairs.

    Go to bed first, a golden purse ;
    Go to bed second, a golden pheasant ;
    Go to bed third, a golden bird !

Go to bed, Tom, go to bed, Tom —
Merry or sober, go to bed, Tom.

———•———

Great A, little a,
Bouncing B!
The cat 's in the cupboard,
And she can't see.

———•———

Great | A was a | larmed at | B's bad be | havior, | "
Be | cause C | D, E, F, de | nied G a | favor. |
H had a | husband with | I, J, | K, and L. |
M married | Mary, and | taught her scholars | how to spell; |
A, B, C, D, | E, F, G, H, | I, J, K, L, | M, N, ||
O, P, Q, R, | S, T, U, V, | Double U, X, Y, Z. ||

———•———

Handy Spandy, Jack-a-dandy,
Loved plum cake and sugar candy;
He bought some at a grocer's shop,
And out he came, hop, hop, hop.

———•———

Hark, hark,
The dogs do bark,
The beggars are coming to town;
Some in rags,
Some in jags,
And some in velvet gowns.

Here goes my lord
A trot, a trot, a trot, a trot,
Here goes my lady
A canter, a canter, a canter, a canter!
Here goes my young master
Jockey-hitch, Jockey-hitch, Jockey-hitch, Jockey-hitch;
Here goes my young miss,
An amble, an amble, an amble, an amble!
The footman lags behind to tipple ale and wine,
And goes gallop, a gallop, a gallop, to make up his time.

———

Here's A, B, C, D, E, F, and G,
H, I, J, K, L, M, N, O, P, Q, R, S, T, U, V,
W, X, Y, and Z.
And O, dear me,[45]
When shall I learn
My A, B, C?

———

Here's A, B, C, D, E, F, and G,
H, I, J, K, L, M, N, O, and P,
Q, R, S, T, U, V, W, X, Y, and Z;
And here is good mamma, who knows
This is the fount whence learning flows.

———

Here sits the Lord Mayor,[46]   [*forehead.*]
Here sit his two men;   [*eyes.*]
Here sits the cock,   [*right cheek.*]
Here sits the hen;   [*left cheek.*]

Here sit the little chickens,   [*tip of nose.*]
Here they run in ;   [*mouth.*]
Chinchopper, chinchopper,
Chinchopper, chin !   [*chuck the chin.*]

Here stands a post :
Who put it there ?
A better man than you ;
Touch it if you dare !

He that would thrive
Must rise at five ;
He that hath thriven
May lie till seven ;
And he that by the plough would thrive,
Himself must either hold or drive.

Hey, my kitten, my kitten,
And hey, my kitten, my deary !
Such a sweet pet as this
Was neither far nor neary.

Here we go up, up, up,
And here we go down, down, downy,
And here we go backwards and forwards,
And here we go round, round, roundy.

Hey, ding a ding, what shall I sing?
How many holes in a skimmer?
Four and twenty, — my stomach is empty;
Pray, mamma, give me some dinner.

————

Sing a song of sixpence,[17]
A pocket full of rye;
Four and twenty blackbirds
Baked in a pie;

When the pie was opened,
The birds began to sing;
Was not that a dainty dish
To set before the king?

The king was in the parlor,
Counting out his money;
The queen was in the kitchen,
Eating bread and honey;

The maid was in the garden,
Hanging out the clothes:
There came a little blackbird,
And snipped off her nose.

Jenny was so mad,
She didn't know what to do;
She put her finger in her ear,
And cracked it right in two.

Hey rub-a-dub, ho rub-a-dub, three maids in a tub,
And what do you think was there?
The butcher, the baker, the candlestick-maker,
And all of them gone to the fair.

———•———

Hick-a-more, Hack-a-more,[48]
On the king's kitchen-door;
All the king's horses,
And all the king's men,
Couldn't drive Hick-a-more, Hack-a-more,
Off the king's kitchen-door.

———•———

Hickery, dickery, 6 and 7,[49]
Alabone, Crackabone, 10 and 11;
Spin, span, muskidan;
Twiddle'um, twaddle'um, 21.

———•———

Hickety, pickety, my black hen,
She lays eggs for gentlemen;
Gentlemen come every day,
To see what my black hen doth lay.

———•———

Hickory, dickory, dock,
The mouse ran up the clock,
The clock struck one,
The mouse ran down;
Hickory, dickory, dock

Hickup, hickup, go away !
Come again another day ;
Hickup, hickup, when I bake,
I'll give to you a butter-cake.

———•———

Higgledy piggledy,[60]
Here we lie,
Picked and plucked,
And put in a pie.
My first is snapping, snarling, growling,
My second 's industrious, romping, and prowling.
Higgledy, piggledy,
Here we lie,
Picked and plucked,
And put in a pie.

———•———

Higglepy, Piggleby,
My black hen,
She lays eggs
For gentlemen ;
Sometimes nine,
And sometimes ten,
Higglepy, Piggleby,
My black hen !

———•———

High, ding, cockatoo-moody,
Make a bed in a barn, I will come to thee ;

High, ding, straps of leather,
Two little puppy-dogs tied together,
One by the head, and one by the tail,
And over the water these puppy-dogs sail.

———•———

Hink, minx! the old witch winks,
    The fat begins to fry;
There's nobody at home but jumping Joan,
    Father, mother, and I.

———•———

    Hot-cross buns!
    Hot-cross buns!
One a penny, two a penny,
    Hot-cross buns!

    Hot-cross buns!
    Hot-cross buns!
If ye have no daughters,
    Give them to your sons.

———•———

How does my lady's garden grow?
How does my lady's garden grow?
With cockle shells, and silver bells,
And pretty maids all of a row.

———•———

How many miles is it to Babylon? —
Threescore miles and ten.

Can I get there by candle-light? —
Yes, and back again!
If your heels are nimble and light,
You may get there by candle-light.

Hub-a-dub dub,
Three men in a tub,
And who do you think they be?
The butcher, the baker,
The candlestick-maker;
Turn 'em out, knaves all three!

Humpty Dumpty sat on a wall,[62]
Humpty Dumpty had a great fall;
Threescore men and threescore more
Cannot place Humpty Dumpty as he was before.

Hush-a-bye, baby,
Daddy is near;
Mammy's a lady,
And that's very clear.

Hush-a-bye, baby, lie still with thy daddy;
Thy mammy has gone to the mill,
To get some wheat, to make some meat,
So pray, my dear baby, lie still.

Hush-a-bye, baby, on the tree-top,
When the wind blows, the cradle will rock ;
When the bough bends, the cradle will fall,
Down will come baby, bough, cradle, and all.

———•———

Hushy, baby, my doll, I pray you don't cry,
And I'll give you some bread and some milk by and by ;
Or perhaps you like custard, or may-be a tart, —
Then to either you're welcome, with all my whole heart.

———•———

1   I am a gold lock.
2   I am a gold key.
1   I am a silver lock.
2   I am a silver key.
1   I am a brass lock.
2   I am a brass key.
1   I am a lead lock.
2   I am a lead key.
1   I am a monk lock.
2   I am a monk key.

———•———

If all the seas were one sea,
What a *great* sea that would be!
And if all the trees were one tree,
What a *great* tree that would be!
And if all the axes were one axe,
What a *great* axe that would be!

And if all the men were one man,
What a *great* man he would be!
And if the *great* man took the *great* axe,
And cut down the *great* tree,
And let it fall into the *great* sea,
What a splish splash *that* would be!

———

If a man who turnips cries,
Cries not when his father dies,
It is a proof that he would rather
Have a turnip than his father.

———

Some little mice sat in a barn to spin;
Pussy came by, and popped her head in;
"Shall I come in, and cut your threads off?"
"O! no, kind sir, you would snap our heads off."

———

If all the world was apple-pie,
    And all the sea was ink,
And all the trees were bread and cheese,
    What should we have for drink?

———

If ifs and ands [53]
Were pots and pans,
There would be no need for tinkers!

4

If I'd as much money as I could spend,
I never would cry old chairs to mend;
Old chairs to mend, old chairs to mend;
I never would cry old chairs to mend.

If I'd as much money as I could tell,
I never would cry old clothes to sell;
Old clothes to sell, old clothes to sell;
I never would cry old clothes to sell.

If wishes were horses,
   Beggars might ride;
If turnips were watches,
   I would wear one by my side.

If you sneeze on Monday, you sneeze for danger;
Sneeze on a Tuesday, kiss a stranger;
Sneeze on a Wednesday, sneeze for a letter;
Sneeze on a Thursday, something better;
Sneeze on a Friday, sneeze for sorrow;
Sneeze on a Saturday, see your sweetheart to-morrow.

I had a little castle upon the sea-side,
   One half was water, the other was land;
I opened my little castle door, and guess what I found;
   I found a fair lady with a cup in her hand.
      The cup was gold, filled with wine;
      Drink, fair lady, and thou shalt be mine.

I had a little cow ;
Hey-diddle, ho-diddle !
I had a little cow, and it had a little calf ;
Hey-diddle, ho-diddle ; and there's my song half.

I had a little cow ;
Hey-diddle, ho-diddle !
I had a little cow, and I drove it to the stall ;
Hey-diddle, ho-diddle ; and there's my song all !

———•———

I had a little dog, and they called him Buff ;
I sent him to the shop for a hap'orth of snuff ;
But he lost the bag and spilled the snuff,
So take that cuff, and that's enough.

———•———

I had a little hen, the prettiest ever seen ;
She washed me the dishes, and kept the house clean ;
She went to the mill to fetch me some flour,
She brought it home in less than an hour ;
She baked me my bread, she brewed me my ale,
She sat by the fire and told many a fine tale.

———•———

I had a little husband,[54]
No bigger than my thumb ;
I put him in a pint pot,
And there I bid him drum.

I bought a little horse,
  That galloped up and down ;
I bridled him, and saddled him,
  And sent him out of town.

I gave him some garters,
  To garter up his hose,
And a little handkerchief
  To wipe his pretty nose.

———•———

I had a little moppet,[54a]
I put it in my pocket,
And fed it with corn and hay ;
  Then came a proud beggar,
  And swore he would have her,
And stole little moppet away.

———•———

I had a little nut-tree ; nothing would it bear[55]
But a silver nutmeg and a golden pear ;
The king of Spain's daughter came to visit me
And all was because of my little nut-tree.
I skipped over water, I danced over sea,
And all the birds in the air couldn't catch me.

———•———

I had a little pony,
  His name was Dapple-gray ;
I lent him to a lady,
  To ride a mile away ;

She whipped him, she slashed him,
    She rode him through the mire;
I would not lend my pony now
    For all the lady's hire.

I had four brothers over the sea;
They each sent a Christmas present to me.
The first sent a cherry without any stone;
The second sent a bird without any bone;
The third sent a blanket without any thread;
The fourth sent a book no man could read.
How *could* there be a cherry without any stone?
How could there be a bird without any bone?
How could there be a blanket without any thread?
How could there be a book no man could read?
When the cherry 's in the blossom it has no stone;
When the bird is in the egg it has no bone;
When the blanket 's in the fleece it has no thread;
When the book is in the press no man can read.

I had two pigeons bright and gay;
They flew from me the other day;
What was the reason they did go?
I cannot tell, for I do not know.

I have a little sister, they call her peep, peep; [56]
She wades the waters deep, deep, deep;
She climbs the mountains high, high, high;
Poor little creature, she has but one eye.

I have been to market, my lady, my lady;
" Then you've not been to the fair," says pussy, says pussy;
I bought me a rabbit, my lady, my lady;
" Then you did not buy a hare," says pussy, says pussy ;
I roasted it, my lady, my lady ;
" Then you did not boil it," says pussy, says pussy ;
I ate it, my lady, my lady ;
" And I'll eat you," says pussy, says pussy.

I'll sing you a song,
Though not very long,
Yet I think it's as pretty as any ;
Put your hand in your purse,
You'll never be worse,
And give the poor singer a penny.

I love my love with an A, because he's Agreeable.[67]
I hate him because he's Avaricious.
He took me to the Sign of the Acorn,
And treated me with Apples.
His name's Andrew,
And he lives at Arlington.

Infir taris,[68]
Inoak noneis.
Inmud eelis,
Inclay noneis.
Goat eativy,
Mare eatoats.

In marble walls as white as milk,[59]
Lined with a skin as soft as silk,
Within a fountain crystal clear,
A golden apple doth appear.
No doors there are to this stronghold,
Yet thieves break in and steal the gold.

———•———

Intery, mintery, cutery-corn,[60]
Apple seed and apple thorn;
Wire brier limber-lock,
Five geese in a flock,
Sit and sing by a spring,
O-u-t, and in again.

———•———

I saw a peacock with a fiery tail,[61]
I saw a blazing comet drop down hail,
I saw a cloud wrapped with ivy round,
I saw an oak creep upon the ground,
I saw a pismire swallow up a whale,
I saw the sea brim-full of ale,
I saw a Venice glass full fifteen feet deep,
I saw a well full of men's tears that weep,
I saw red eyes all of a flaming fire,
I saw a house bigger than the moon and higher,
I saw the sun at twelve o'clock at night,
I saw the man that saw this wondrous sight.

I saw a ship a-sailing,
  A-sailing on the sea ;
And O ! it was all laden
  With pretty things for thee !

There were comfits in the cabin,
  And apples in the hold ;
The sails were made of silk,
  And the masts were made of gold !

The four and twenty sailors,
  That stood between the decks,
Were four and twenty white mice,
  With chains about their necks.

The captain was a duck,
  With a packet on his back ;
And when the ship began to move,
  The captain said, " Quack ! quack ! "

———•———

Is John Smith within ? —
Yes, that he is.
Can he set a shoe ? —
Aye, marry, two ;
Here a nail, and there a nail,
Tick, tack, too.

The fox and his wife they had a great strife,
They never ate mustard in all their whole life;
They ate their meat without fork or knife,
    And loved to be picking a bone, e-ho!

The fox jumped up on a moonlight night;
The stars they were shining, and all things bright;
" O ho!" said the fox, " it's a very fine night
    For me to go through the town, e-ho!"

The fox, when he came to yonder stile,
He lifted his lugs[62] and he listened a while!
" O ho!" said the fox, " it's but a short mile
    From this unto yonder wee town, e-ho!"

The fox, when he came to the farmer's gate,
Who should he see but the farmer's drake;
" I love you well for your master's sake,
    And long to be picking your bone, e-ho!"

The gray goose she ran round the hay-stack,
" O ho!" said the fox, " you are very fat;
You'll grease my beard, and ride on my back
    From this unto yonder wee town, e-ho!"

Old Gammer Hipple-hopple hopped out of bed,
She opened the casement, and popped out her head;
" O husband! O husband! the gray goose is dead,
    And the fox has gone through the town, O!"

Then the old man got up in his red cap,
And swore he would catch the fox in a trap;
But the fox was too cunning, and gave him the slip,
    And ran through the town, the town, O!

When he got to the top of the hill,
He blew his trumpet both loud and shrill,
For joy that he was safe
    Through the town, O!

When the fox came back to his den,
He had young ones both nine and ten,
'You're welcome home, daddy, you may go again,
If you bring us such nice meat
    From the town, O!"

———•———

It's once I courted as pretty a lass
    As ever your eyes did see;
But now she's come to such a pass,
    She never will do for me.
She invited me to her own house,
    Where oft I'd been before,
And she tumbled me into the hog-tub,
    And I'll never go there any more.

———•———

I went into my grandmother's garden,[a]
And there I found a farthing.

I went into my next-door neighbor's,
There I bought a pipkin and a popkin,
A slipkin and a slopkin,
A nail-board, a sail-board,
And all for a farthing.

———•———

I went to the toad that lies under the wall;[64]
I charmed him out, and he came at my call;
I scratched out the eyes of the owl before,
I tore the bat's wing; what would you have more?

———•———

I went to the wood and got it;[65]
I sat me down and looked at it;
The more I looked at it the less I liked it,
And I brought it home because I couldn't help it.

———•———

1. I went up one pair of stairs.
2. Just like me.
1. I went up two pair of stairs.
2. Just like me.
1. I went into a room.
2. Just like me.
1. I looked out of a window.
2. Just like me.
1. And there I saw a monkey.
2. Just like me.

I won't be my father's Jack,
   I won't be my mother's Gill,
I will be the fiddler's wife,
   And have music when I will.
      T'other little tune,
      T'other little tune,
      Pr'ythee, love, play me
      T'other little tune.

———•———

I would if I could,
If I couldn't, how could I ?
I couldn't without I could, could I ?
Could you, without you could, could ye ?
Could ye, could ye ?
Could you, without you could, could ye ?

———•———

Jack and Jill went up the hill,
   To fetch a pail of water ;
Jack fell down, and broke his crown,
   And Jill came tumbling after.

———•———

Jack be nimble,
   And Jack be quick ;
And Jack jump over
   The candlestick.

Jacky, come, give me thy fiddle,
  If ever thou mean to thrive;
Nay; I'll not give my fiddle
  To any man alive.

If I should give my fiddle,
  They'll think that I'm gone mad;
For many a joyful day
  My fiddle and I have had.

Jack in the pulpit, out and in;
Sold his wife for a minikin pin.

Jack Sprat
Had a cat,
It had but one ear;
It went to buy butter
When butter was dear.

Jack Sprat could eat no fat,[68]
  His wife could eat no lean;
Betwixt them both, they cleared the plate,
  And licked the platter clean.

Jack Sprat's pig,
He was not very little,

Nor yet very big;
He was not very lean,
He was not very fat;
He'll do well for a grunt,
Says little Jack Sprat.

———•———

Jeanie, come tie my,
Jeanie, come tie my,
Jeanie, come tie my bonnie cravat;
I've tied it behind,
I've tied it before,
And I've tied it so often, I'll tie it no more.

———•———

Jemmy Jed went into a shed,
   And made a ted of straw his bed;
An owl came out and flew about,
   And Jemmy Jed up stakes and fled.
Wasn't Jemmy Jed a staring fool,
Born in the woods, to be scared by an owl?

———•———

Jim and George were two great lords,
   They fought all in a churn;
And when that Jim got George by the nose,
   Then George began to girn.

———•———

" John, come, sell thy fiddle,
   And buy thy wife a gown.'

"No, I'll not sell my fiddle,
For ne'er a wife in town."

Jenny Wren fell sick upon a merry time,
In came Robin Redbreast, and brought her sops and wine.
"Eat well of the sop, Jenny, drink well of the wine;"
"Thank you, Robin, you shall be mine."
Then Jenny she got well, and stood upon her feet,
And told Robin plainly she loved him not a bit.

Robin, being angry, hopped upon a twig,
Saying, "Out upon you, fie upon you, bold-faced jig!"
Jenny Wren fell sick again, and Jenny Wren did die;
The doctors vowed they'd cure her, or know the reason
    why.

Doctor Hawk felt her pulse, and shaking his head,
Says, "I fear I can't save her, because she's quite dead."
"She'll do very well," says sly Doctor Fox;
"If she takes but one pill from out of this box"

With hartshorn in hand came Doctor Tomtit,
Saying, "Really, good sirs, it's only a fit."
"You're right, Doctor Tit, the truth I've no doubt of;
But death is a fit folks seldom get out of."

Doctor Cat says, "Indeed, I don't think she's dead;
I believe, if I try, she yet might be bled."

"I think, Puss, you're foolish," then says Doctor Goose,
"For to bleed a dead Wren can be of no use."

Doctor Owl then declared that the cause of her death,
He really believed, was the want of more breath.
"Indeed, Doctor Owl, you are much in the right;
You might as well have said the day is not night."

Says Robin, "Get out! you're a parcel of quacks;
Or I'll lay this good stick on each of your backs."
Then Robin began to bang them about;
They stayed for no fees, but were glad to get out.

———+———

John Cook had a little gray mare; he, haw, hum!
Her back stood up, and her bones were bare; he, haw, hum!

John Cook was riding up Shuter's bank; he, haw, hum!
And there his nag did kick and prank; he, haw, hum!
John Cook was riding up Shuter's hill; he, haw, hum!
His mare fell down, and she made her will; he, haw, hum!

The bridle and saddle were laid on the shelf; he, haw, hum!
If you want any more you may sing it yourself; he, haw, hum!

———+———

Johnny shall have a new bonnet,
And Johnny shall go to the fair,
And Johnny shall have a blue ribbon
To tie up his bonny brown hair.

And why may not I love Johnny?
　And why may not Johnny love me?
And why may not I love Johnny
　As well as another body?
And here's a leg for a stocking,
　And here's a leg for a shoe;
And he has a kiss for his daddy,
　And two for his mammy, I trow.
And why may not I love Johnny?
　And why may not Johnny love me?
And why may not I love Johnny
　As well as another body?

———

The Sow came in with the saddle,
The little Pig rocked the cradle,
The Dish jumped on the table,
To see the Pot swallow the Ladle.
The Spit that stood behind the door
Threw the Pudding-stick on the floor.
"Odsplut!" said the Gridiron, "can't you agree?
I'm the head constable, — bring them to me."

———

Johnny Armstrong killed a calf,
Peter Henderson got the half,
Willy Wilkinson got the head:
Ring the bell, the calf is dead!
5

Lavender blue and Rosemary green,[68]
When I am king you shall be queen ;
Call up my maids at four of the clock,
Some to the wheel, and some to the rock,[68]
Some to make hay, and some to thresh corn,
And you and I will keep the bed warm.

———

Lady bird, lady bird, fly away home,
Thy house is on fire, thy children all gone,
All but one, and her name is Ann,
And she crept under the pudding-pan.

———

Lazy Tom, with jacket blue,
Stole his father's gouty shoe.
The worst of harm that dad can wish him,
Is that his gouty shoe may fit him.

———

Leg over leg,
    As the dog went to Dover ;
When he came to a stile,
    Jump he went over.

———

" Lend me thy mare to ride a mile ? "
" She is lamed, leaping over a stile."
" Alack ! and I must keep the fair !
I'll give thee money for thy mare."

"O, O! say you so?
Money will make the mare to go!"

————.

1 Let us go to the wood, says this pig;[70]
2 What to do there? says that pig;
3 To look for my mother, says this pig;
4 What to do with her? says that pig;
5 Kiss her to death, says this pig.

————

Little Betty Blue
Lost her holiday shoe;
What can little Betty do?
Give her another
To match the other,
And then she may walk in two.

————

Little blue Betty lived in a den,
She sold good ale to gentlemen:
Gentlemen came there every day,
And little blue Betty hopped away.
She hopped up-stairs to make her bed,
And she tumbled down and broke her head.

————

Little Bo-peep has lost her sheep,[71]
And can't tell where to find them;

Leave them alone, and they'll come home,
  And bring their tails behind them.

Little Bo-peep fell fast asleep,
  And dreamed she heard them bleating;
But when she awoke, she found it a joke,
  For they were still a-fleeting.

Then up she took her little crook,
  Determined for to find them;
She found them indeed, but it made her heart bleed,
  For they'd left all their tails behind 'em.

———

Little boy blue, come blow up your horn,
The sheep's in the meadow, the cow's in the corn;
Where's the little boy that tends the sheep?
He's under the hay-cock, fast asleep.
Go wake him, go wake him. O! no, not I;
For if I awake him, he'll certainly cry.

———

Little Dicky Dilver
Had a wife of silver;
He took a stick and broke her back,
And threw her in the river.
Fine stockings, fine shoes,
Fine yellow hair,
Double ruffle round her neck
And not a dress to wear.

Little General Monk[72]
Sat upon a trunk,
Eating a crust of bread ;
There fell a hot coal,
And burnt in his clothes a hole,
Now General Monk is dead.
Keep always from the fire ;
If it catch your attire,
You, too, like Monk, will be dead.

———

Little girl, little girl, where have you been?
Gathering roses to give to the queen.
Little girl, little girl, what gave she you?
She gave me a diamond as big as my shoe.

———

Little Jack-a-Dandy
Wanted sugar candy,
And fairly for it cried ;
But little Bill Cook,
Who always read his book,
Shall have a horse to ride.

———

Little Jack Dandy-prat was my first suitor:
He had a dish and a spoon, and he'd some pewter ;
He'd linen and woolen, and woolen and linen,
A little pig in a string cost him five shilling.

Little Jack Horner sat in the corner,[73]
Eating a Christmas pie ;
He put in his thumb, and he took out a plum,
And said, " What a good boy am I ! "

———·———

Little Jack Jingle,
He used to live single ;
But when he got tired of this kind of life,
He left off being single, and lived with his wife.

———·———

Little Jack Nory
Told me a story.
How he tried
Cock-horse to ride,
Sword and scabbard by his side,
Saddle, leaden spurs and switches,
His pocket tight
With pence all bright,
Marbles, tops, puzzles, props,
Now he's put in a jacket and breeches.

———·———

Little John Jiggy Jag,
He rode a penny nag,
And went to Wigan to woo ; [74]
When he came to a beck,[75]
He fell and broke his neck, —
Johnny, how dost thou now ?

I made him a hat,
Of my coat-lap,
And stockings of pearly blue ;
A hat and a feather,
To keep out cold weather ;
So, Johnny, how dost thou now ?

Little Johnny Pringle had a little pig ;
It was very little, so was not very big.
As it was playing beneath the shed,
In half a minute poor Piggie was dead.
So Johnny Pringle he sat down and cried,
And Betty Pringle she laid down and died.
There is the history of one, two, and three,
Johnny Pringle, Betty Pringle, and Piggie Wiggie.

Little King Boggen he built a fine hall,
Pie-crust and pastry-crust, that was the wall ;
The windows were made of black puddings and white,
And slated with pancakes — you ne'er saw the like.

Little maid, pretty maid, whither goest thou ?
" Down in the forest to milk my cow."
Shall I go with thee ? " No, not now ;
When I send for thee, then come thou."

Little Miss Muffett
She sat on a tuffett,[76]
Eating of curds and whey;
There came a black spider,
And sat down beside her,
Which frightened Miss Muffett away.

————

Little Nancy Etticoat,[77]
In a white petticoat,
  And a red nose;
The longer she stands,
  The shorter she grows.

————

Little Poll Parrot
Sat in her garret,
Eating toast and tea;
  A little brown mouse,
  Jumped into the house,
And stole it all away.

————

Little Robin Redbreast
  Sat upon a rail;
Niddle naddle went his head,
  Wiggle waggle went his tail.

————

Little Robin Redbreast sat upon a tree,
Up went Pussy cat, and down went he;

Down came Pussy cat, and away Robin ran ;
Says little Robin Redbreast, "Catch me if you can."

Little Robin Redbreast jumped upon a wall,
Pussy cat jumped after him, and almost got a fall,
Little Robin chirped and sang, and what did Pussy say ?
Pussy cat said " Mew," and Robin jumped away.

There was a little man,
And he had a little gun,
And his bullets were made of lead, lead, lead ;
He went to the brook,
And saw a little duck,
And shot it through the head, head, head.
He carried it home
To his old wife Joan,
And bade her a fire to make, make, make,
To roast the little duck
He had shot in the brook,
And he'd go and fetch the drake, drake, drake.

Little Tee Wee,
He went to sea
In an open boat ;
And while afloat
The little boat bended,
And my story's ended.

Little Tommy Grace,
Had a pain in his face,
So bad that he could not learn a letter;
When in came Dicky Long,
Singing such a funny song,
That Tommy laughed, and found his face much better.

———

Little Tommy Tittlemouse
Lived in a little house;
He caught fishes
In other men's ditches.

———

Little Tom Tittlemouse,
Lived in a bell-house;
The bell-house broke,
And Tom Tittlemouse woke.

———

Little Tommy Tucker,
Sing for your supper.
What shall I sing?
White bread and butter.

How shall I cut it
Without any knife?
How shall I marry
Without any wife?

Lives in winter.[78]
Dies in summer,
And grows with its root upwards!

———•———

London bridge is broken down,
  Dance o'er my lady Lee;
London bridge is broken down,
  With a gay lady.

How shall we build it up again?
  Dance o'er my lady Lee;
How shall we build it up again?
  With a gay lady.

Silver and gold will be stole away,
  Dance o'er my lady Lee;
Silver and gold will be stole away,
  With a gay lady.

Build it up again with iron and steel,
  Dance o'er my lady Lee;
Build it up with iron and steel,
  With a gay lady.

Iron and steel will bend and bow,
  Dance o'er my lady Lee;
Iron and steel will bend and bow
  With a gay lady.

Build it up with wood and clay,
  Dance o'er my lady Lee :
Build it up with wood and clay,
  With a gay lady.

Wood and clay will wash away,
  Dance o'er my lady Lee ;
Wood and clay will wash away,
  With a gay lady.

Build it up with stone so strong,
  Dance o'er my lady Lee ;
Huzza ! 'twill last for ages long,
  With a gay lady.

  Long legs, crooked thighs,
  Little head, and no eyes.

Love your own, kiss your own,
  Love your own mother, hinny,
For if she was dead and gone,
  You'd ne'er get such another, hinny.

  Made in London,
  Sold at York,
  Stops a bottle,
  And *is* a cork.

Make three-fourths of a cross,[50]
  And a circle complete ;
And let two semicircles
  On a perpendicular meet ;
Next add a triangle
  That stands on two feet ;
Next two semicircles,
  And a circle complete.

———•———

Margery Mutton-pie and Johnny Bopeep,
They met together in Grace-church street ;
In and out, in and out, over the way,
O ! says Johnny, 'tis chop-nose day.

———•———

Master I have, and I am his man,
  Gallop a dreary dun ;
Master I have, and I am his man,
And I'll get a wife as fast as I can ;
With a heighly, gaily, gamberally,
Higgledy, piggledy, niggledy, niggledy,
  Gallop a dreary dun.

———•———

Matthew, Mark, Luke, and John[51]
Guard the bed that I lay on !
Four corners to my bed,
Four angels round my head ;
One to watch, one to pray,
And two to bear my soul away.

Milkman, Milkman, where have you been?
In Buttermilk Channel up to my chin;
I spilt my milk, and spoilt my clothes,
And got a long icicle to my nose.

Miss Jane had a bag, and a mouse was in it,
She opened the bag, he was out in a minute,
The cat saw him jump, and run under the table,
And the dog said, Catch him, puss, soon as you're able.

Mistress Mary, quite contra'ry,[82]
How does your garden grow?
With cockle-shells, and silver bells,
And pretty maids all in a row.

Mollie, my sister, and I fell out,
And what do you think it was about?
She loved coffee, and I loved tea,[83]
And that was the reason we couldn't agree.

Moss was a little man, and a little mare did buy;
For kicking and for sprawling, none her could come nigh;
She could trot, she could amble, and could canter here and
      there,
But one night she strayed away — so Moss lost his mare.

Moss got up next morning to catch her fast asleep,
And round about the frosty fields so nimbly he did creep,
Dead in a ditch he found her, and glad to find her there ;
So I'll tell you by and by, how Moss caught his mare.

"Rise! stupid, rise!" he thus to her did say ;
"Arise, you beast, you drowsy beast, get up without delay,
For I must ride you to the town, so don't lie sleeping there ;
He put the halter round her neck — so Moss caught his mare.

Multiplication is vexation,[34]
  Division is as bad ;
The Rule of Three doth puzzle me,
  And Practice drives me mad.

My dear, do you know,
  How a long time ago,
Two poor little children,
  Whose names I don't know,
Were stolen away on a fine summer's day,
And left in a wood, as I've heard people say.

And when it was night,
  So sad was their plight,
The sun it went down,
  And the moon gave no light !
They sobbed, and they sighed, and they bitterly cried,
And the poor little things, they lay down and died.

And when they were dead,
The Robins so red
Brought strawberry leaves,
And over them spread;
And all the day long,
They sung them this song:
" Poor babes in the wood! poor babes in the wood!
And don't you remember the babes in the wood?"

———————

My father he died, but I can't tell you how,
He left me six horses to drive in my plough;
    With my wing, wang, waddle O,
    Jack sing saddle O,
    Blowsey boys bubble O,
        Under the broom.

I sold my six horses, and bought me a cow,
I'd fain have made a fortune, but did not know how;
    With my, etc.

I sold my cow, and I bought me a calf;
I'd fain have made a fortune, but lost the best half;
    With my, etc.

I sold my calf, and I bought me a cat;
A pretty thing she was, in my chimney sat;
    With my, etc.

I sold my cat, and bought me a mouse;
He carried fire in his tail, and burnt down my house:
    With my, etc.

There was a piper had a cow,
  And he'd no hay to give her.
He took his pipe, and played a tune,
  Consider, cow, consider !

The cow considered very well,
  For she gave the piper a penny,
That he might play the tune again,
  Of " Corn rigs are bonnie ! "

———

My father was a Frenchman,[85]
  He bought me a fiddle ;
He cut me here, he cut me here,
  He cut me right in the middle.

———

My grandmother sent me a new-fashioned three-cornered
cambric country-cut handkerchief.   Not an old-fashioned
three-cornered cambric country-cut handkerchief, but a new-
fashioned three-cornered cambric country-cut handkerchief.

———

My little old man and I fell out,
I'll tell you what 'twas all about :
I had money and he had none,
And that's the way the row begun.
  6

My maid Mary
She minds her dairy,
While I go hoeing and mowing each morn,
Merrily run the reel
And the little spinning-wheel,
Whilst I am singing and mowing my corn.

———·———

My story's ended,
My spoon is bended :
If you don't like it,
. Go to the next door,
And get it mended.

———·———

My true love lives far from me,[66]
Perrie, Merrie, Dixie, Dominie.
Many a rich present he sends to me,
Petrum, Partrum, Paradise, Temporie,
Perrie, Merrie, Dixie, Dominie.

He sent me a goose without a bone ;
He sent me a cherry without a stone.
Petrum, etc.

He sent me a Bible no man could read ;
He sent me a blanket without a thread.
Petrum, etc.

How could there be a goose without a bone?
How could there be a cherry without a stone?
    Petrum, etc.

How could there be a Bible no man could read?
How could there be a blanket without a thread?
    Petrum, etc.

When the goose is in the egg-shell, there is no bone;
When the cherry is in the blossom, there is no stone.
    Petrum, etc.

When the Bible is in the press, no man it can read;
When the wool is on the sheep's back, there is no thread.
    Petrum, etc.

————

Nature requires five,
    Custom gives seven!
Laziness takes nine,
    And wickedness eleven.

————

Naughty Willy Bell
Fell into the well,
Though mamma told him not to move its cover;
    For this stubborn little elf
    Only chose to please himself.
Looking in, he turned giddy, and fell over.

But the gardener heard him shout,
And with assistance got him out;
You never saw a boy in such a mess;
In future he will find Mamma he'd better mind,
Nor again ever cause her such distress.

———

Needles and pins, needles and pins,
When a man marries, his trouble begins.

———

Nose, nose, jolly red nose,[57]
   And what gave you that jolly red nose?
Nutmegs and cinnamon, spices and cloves,
   And they gave me this jolly red nose.

———

Number, number nine, this hoop's mine;
Number, number ten, take it back again.

———

O! mother, I shall be married to Mr. Punchinello.
To Mr. Punch,
To Mr. Joe,
To Mr. Nell,
To Mr. Lo,
Mr. Punch, Mr. Joe,
Mr. Nell; Mr. Lo,
To Mr. Punchinello.

Of all the gay birds that e'er I did see,[88]
The owl is the fairest by far to me;
For all the day long she sits on a tree,
And when the night comes, away flies she.

————

O, where are you going,[89]
  My pretty maiden fair,
With your red rosy cheeks,
  And your coal-black hair ?
" I'm going a-milking,
  Kind sir," says she ;
" And it's dabbling in the dew,
  Where you'll find me."

May I go with you,
  My pretty maiden fair, etc.
" O, you may go with me,
  Kind sir," says she, etc.

If I should chance to kiss you,
  My pretty maiden fair, etc.
" The wind may take it off again,
  Kind sir," says she, etc.

And what is your father,
  My pretty maiden fair, etc.
" My father is a farmer,
  Kind sir," says she, etc.

And what is your mother,
   My pretty maiden fair, etc.
" My mother is a dairy-maid,
   Kind sir," says she, etc.

And what is your sweetheart,
   My pretty maiden fair, etc.
" William the carpenter,
   Kind sir," says she, etc.

———

Old Father Graybeard,
   Without tooth or tongue,
If you'll give me your finger,
   I'll give you my thumb.

———

Old King Cole[90]
Was a merry old soul,
And a merry old soul was he ;
He called for his pipe,
And he called for his bowl,
And he called for his fiddlers three.
Every fiddler, he had a fiddle,
And a very fine fiddle had he ;
Twee tweedle dee, tweedle dee, went the fiddlers.
   O, there's none so rare,
   As can compare
With King Cole and his fiddlers three !

Old Mistress McShuttle
Lived in a coal-scuttle,
Along with her dog and her cat :
  What they ate I can't tell,
  But 'tis known very well,
That none of the party were fat.

———

Old Mother Goose, when [91]
  She wanted to wander,
Would ride through the air
  On a very fine gander.

Mother Goose had a house,
  'Twas built in a wood,
Where an owl at the door
  For sentinel stood.

This is her son Jack,
  A plain-looking lad ;
He is not very good,
  Nor yet very bad.

She sent him to market,
  A live goose he bought,
" Here, Mother," says he,
  " It will not go for nought.'

Jack's goose and her gander
  Grew very fond ;

They'd both eat together,
    Or swim in one pond.

Jack found one morning,
    As I have been told,
His goose had laid him
    An egg of pure gold.

Jack rode to his mother,
    The news for to tell;
She called him a good boy,
    And said it was well.

Jack sold his gold egg
    To a rogue of a Jew,
Who cheated him out of
    The half of his due.

Then Jack went a-courting
    A lady so gay,
As fair as the lily,
    And sweet as the May.

The Jew and the Squire
    Came behind his back,
And began to belabor
    The sides of poor Jack.

The old Mother Goose
    That instant came in,

And turned her son Jack
  Into famed Harlequin.

She then, with her wand,
  Touched the lady so fine,
And turned her at once
  Into sweet Columbine.

The gold egg into the sea
  Was thrown then, —
When Jack jumped in,
  And got the egg back again.

The Jew got the goose,
  Which he vowed he would kill,
Resolving at once
  His pockets to fill.

Jack's Mother came in,
  And caught the goose soon,
And, mounting its back,
  Flew up to the moon.

———•———

Old Mother Hubbard[92]
Went to the cupboard,
  To get her poor dog a bone ;
But when she came there,
The cupboard was bare,
  And so the poor dog had none.

She went to the baker's
　To buy him some bread ;
But when she came back,
　The poor dog was dead.

She went to the joiner's
　To buy him a coffin ;
But when she came back,
　The poor dog was laughing.

She took a clean dish
　To get him some tripe ;
But when she came back,
　He was smoking his pipe.

She went to the fishmonger's
　To buy him some fish ;
And when she came back,
　He was licking the dish.

She went to the ale-house
　To get him some beer ;
But when she came back,
　The dog sat in a chair.

She went to the tavern
　For white wine and red ;
But when she came back,
　The dog stood on his head.

She went to the hatter's
  To buy him a hat;
But when she came back,
  He was feeding the cat.

She went to the barber's
  To buy him a wig;
But when she came back,
  He was dancing a jig.

She went to the fruiterer's
  To buy him some fruit;
But when she came back,
  He was playing the flute.

She went to the tailor's
  To buy him a coat;
But when she came back,
  He was riding a goat.

She went to the cobbler's
  To buy him some shoes;
But when she came back,
  He was reading the news.

She went to the seamstress
  To buy him some linen;
But when she came back,
  The dog was spinning.

She went to the hosier's
  To buy him some hose;
But when she came back,
  He was dressed in his clothes.

The dame made a curtsy,
  The dog made a bow;
The dame said, Your servant,
  The dog said, Bow, wow.

One day an old cat and her kittens
Put on their bonnets and mittens,
And as it was damp, why, they put on their clogs;
They thought it would be very nice
To go out in search of some mice, —
But they ran home again when they saw two fierce dogs

Old Mother Twitchett had but one eye,[93]
And a long tail which she let fly;
And every time she went over a gap,
She left a bit of her tail in a trap.

Old woman, old woman, shall we go a shearing?
"Speak a little louder, sir, I am very thick of hearing."
Old woman, old woman, shall I love you dearly?
"Thank you, kind sir, I hear you very clearly."

Three little kittens lost their mittens,
  And they began to cry :
O mother dear, we very much fear
That we have lost our mittens.

" Lost your mittens, you naughty kittens !
  Then you shall have no pie."
    Mee-ow, mee-ow, mee-ow !
And we can have no pie.
    Mee-ow, mee-ow, mee-ow !

Once in my life I married a wife,
  And where do you think I found her ?
On Gretna Green, in a velvet sheen,
  And I took up a stick to pound her.
She jumped over a barberry-bush,
  And I jumped over a timber :
I showed her a gay gold ring,
  And she showed me her finger.

Once I saw a little bird
  Come hop, hop, hop ;
So I cried, " Little bird,
  Will you stop, stop, stop ? "
And was going to the window
  To say, " How do you do ? "
But he shook his little tail,
  And far away he flew.

One-ery, two-ery, hickary, hum,[94]
Fillison, follison, Nicholas, John,
Quever, quauver, Irish Mary,
Stenkarum, stankerum, buck!

One-ery, two-ery,[95]
   Ziccary, zan;
Hollow bone, crack a bone,
   Ninery ten;
Spittery, spot,
   It must be done;
Twiddleum, twaddleum,
   Twenty-one.
Hink, spink, the puddings stink,
   The fat begins to fry;
Nobody at home, but jumping Joan,
   Father, mother, and I.
Stick, stock, stone dead,
   Blind man can't see,
Every knave will have a slave,
   You or I must be he.

One misty, moisty morning,[96]
   When cloudy was the weather,
I chanced to meet an old man
   Clothed all in leather;
He began to compliment,
   And I began to grin, —

"How do you do," and "How do you do,"
And "How do you do" again!

One moonshiny night⁹ʳ
As I sat high,
Waiting for one
To come by;
The boughs did bend,
My heart did ache
To see what a hole the fox did make.

One old Oxford ox opening oysters;
Two tee-totums totally tired of trying to trot to Tadbury;
Three tall tigers tippling tenpenny tea;
Four fat friars fanning fainting flies;
Five frippy Frenchmen foolishly fishing for flies;
Six sportsmen shooting snipes;
Seven Severn salmons swallowing shrimps;
Eight Englishmen eagerly examining Europe;
Nine nimble noblemen nibbling nonpareils;
Ten tinkers tinkling upon ten tin tinder-boxes with tenpenny
        tacks;
Eleven elephants elegantly equipped;
Twelve typographical topographers typically translating types.

One's none;
Two's some;

Three's a many
Four's a penny;
Five is a little hundred.

———◆———

One to make ready,[38]
And two to prepare;
Good luck to the rider,
And away goes the mare.

———◆———

One, two,
Buckle my shoe;
Three, four,
Shut the door;
Five, six,
Pick up sticks;
Seven, eight,
Lay them straight;
Nine, ten,
A good fat hen;
Eleven, twelve,
Who will delve?
Thirteen, fourteen,
Maids a-courting;
Fifteen, sixteen,
Maids a-kissing;
Seventeen, eighteen,
Maids a-waiting;
Nineteen, twenty,
My stomach's empty.

One, two, three,
I love coffee,
And Billy loves tea,
How good you be !
One, two, three,
I love coffee,
And Billy loves tea.

———

O rare Harry Parry,
When will you marry ?
" When apples and pears are ripe."
I'll come to your wedding,
Without any bidding,
And dance and sing all the night.

———

1, 2, 3, 4, 5 !
I caught a hare alive ;
6, 7, 8, 9, 10 !
I let her go again.

———

On Saturday night,
Shall be all my care
To powder my locks
And curl my hair.

7

On Sunday morning
My love will come in,
When he will marry me
With a gold ring.

O that I was where I would be,
Then would I be where I am not!
But where I am I must be,
And where I would be I cannot.

O the little rusty, dusty, rusty miller!
I'll not change my wife for either gold or siller.

Our saucy boy, Dick,
Had a nice little stick
Cut from a hawthorn tree;
And with this pretty stick,
He thought he could beat
A boy much bigger than he.

But the boy turned round,
And hit him a rebound,
Which did so frighten poor Dick,
That, without more delay,
He ran quite away,
And over a hedge he jumped quick.

Over the water and over the lea,[99]
And over the water to Charley.
Charley loves good ale and wine,
And Charley loves good brandy,
And Charley loves a pretty girl,
As sweet as sugar-candy.

Over the water and over the sea,
And over the water to Charley.
I'll have none of your nasty beef,
Nor I'll have none of your barley;
But I'll have some of your very best flour,
To make a white cake for my Charley.

———•———

Pat-a cake, pat-a-cake, baker's man!
So I will, master, as fast as I can:
Pat it, and prick it, and mark it with T,
Put it in the oven for [*Tommy*] and me.

———•———

Pease-porridge hot, pease-porridge cold,
Pease-porridge in the pot, nine days old.
Spell me *that* without a P,
And a clever scholar you will be.

———•———

Pease-pudding hot,[100]
Pease-pudding cold,
Pease-pudding in the pot,
Nine days old.

Some like it hot,
 Some like it cold,
 Some like it in the pot,
 Nine days old.

———•———

Pemmy was a pretty girl,
 But Fanny was a better;
Pemmy looked like any churl,
 When little Fanny let her.

Pemmy had a pretty nose,
 But Fanny had a better;
Pemmy oft would come to blows,
 But Fanny would not let her.

Pemmy had a pretty doll,
 But Fanny had a better;
Pemmy chattered like a poll,
 When little Fanny let her.

Pemmy had a pretty song,
 But Fanny had a better;
Pemmy would sing all day long,
 But Fanny would not let her.

Pemmy loved a pretty lad,
 And Fanny loved a better;
And Pemmy wanted for to wed,
 But Fanny would not let her.

Peter, Peter, pumpkin-eater,
Had a wife, and couldn't keep her ;
He put her in a pumpkin-shell,
And there he kept her very well.

Peter, Peter, pumpkin-eater,
Had another and didn't love her ;
Peter learned to read and spell,
And then he loved her very well.

———•———

Peter Piper picked a peck of pickled peppers ;
A peck of pickled peppers Peter Piper picked ;
If Peter Piper picked a peck of pickled peppers,
Where's the peck of pickled peppers Peter Piper picked *

———•———

Peter White will ne'er go right, [101]
    Would you know the reason why ?
He follows his nose wherever he goes.
    And that stands all awry,

———•———

Please to remember [102]
    The fifth of November,
Gunpowder, treason, and plot :
    I know no reason
    Why gunpowder treason
Should ever be forgotten.

Poor old Robinson Crusoe![103]
Poor old Robinson Crusoe!
They made him a coat
Of an old nanny-goat,
I wonder how they could do so!
With a ring-a-ting tang,
And a ring-a-ting tang,
Poor old Robinson Crusoe!

————

Polly, put the kettle on,
Polly, put the kettle on,
Polly, put the kettle on,
    And let's drink tea.

Sukey, take it off again,
Sukey, take it off again,
Sukey, take it off again,
    They're all gone away.

————

Punch and Judy
    Fought for a pie;
Punch gave Judy
    A sad blow on the eye.

————

Pussy-cat, wussy-cat, with a white foot,
When is your wedding? for I'll come to't.
The beer's to brew, the bread's to bake,
Pussy-cat, pussy-cat, don't be too late.

Pussy-cat eat the dumplings, the dumplings,
Pussy-cat eat the dumplings.
   Mamma stood by,
   And cried, " O, fie!
Why did you eat the dumplings?"

Pussy-cat Mole
Jumped over a coal,
   And in her best petticoat burnt a great hole.
Poor pussy's weeping, she'll have no more milk,
Until her best petticoat's mended with silk.

Pussy-cat, pussy-cat, where have you been?
"I've been up to London to look at the queen."
Pussy-cat, pussy-cat, what did you there?
"I frightened a little mouse under the chair."

   Rain, rain, go away,
   Come again another day;
   Little [*Arthur*] wants to play.

   Riddle me, riddle me, ree,
   A hawk sat upon a tree;
   And he says to himself, says he,
   "O dear! what a fine bird I be!"

Rigadoon, rigadoon, now let him fly,
Sit upon mother's foot, jump him up high.

———

Ring the bell! [*giving a lock of the hair a pull.*] [104]
Knock at the door! [*tapping the forehead.*]
Draw the latch! [*pulling up the nose.*]
And walk in! [*opening the mouth and putting in the finger.*]

———

Ride a cock-horse to Banbury-cross
To see an old lady upon a white horse,
Rings on her fingers, and bells on her toes,
And so she makes music wherever she goes.

———

Ride a cock-horse to Banbury-cross,
To buy little Johnny a galloping horse;
It trots behind, and it ambles before,
And Johnny shall ride till he can ride no more.

———

Ride a cock-horse to Banbury-cross,
To see what Tommy can buy;
A penny white loaf, a penny white cake,
And a two-penny apple-pie.

Ride, baby, ride,
Pretty baby shall ride,
And have a little puppy-dog tied to her side,
And little pussy-cat tied to the other,
And away she shall ride to see her grandmother,
To see her grandmother,
To see her grandmother.

———•———

Three wise men of Gotham [105]
Went to sea in a bowl;
And if the bowl had been stronger,
My song would have been longer.

———•———

Robbin the Bobbin, the big-bellied Ben,
He eat more meat than fourscore men;
He eat a cow, he eat a calf,
He eat a butcher and a half;
He eat a church, he eat a steeple,
He eat the priest and all the people!

———•———

" Robert Barnes, fellow fine,
Can you shoe this horse of mine?"
" Yes, good sir, that I can,
As well as any other man:
Here a nail, and there a prod, [106]
And now, good sir, your horse is shod."

Robert Rowley rolled a round roll round,
A round roll Robert Rowley rolled round;
Where rolled the round roll Robert Rowley rolled round?

———

Robin and Richard were two pretty men;
They laid in bed till the clock struck ten;
Then up starts Robin, and looks at the sky;
"Oho! brother Richard, the sun's very high."

———

Rock-a-bye, baby, thy cradle is green;
Father's a nobleman, mother's a queen;
And Betty's a lady, and wears a gold ring;
And Johnny's a drummer, and drums for the king.

———

Rompty-iddity, row, row, row,
If I had a good supper, I could eat it now.

———

Rosemary green
    And lavender blue,
Thyme and sweet marjorum,
    Hyssop and rue.

———

Round about, round about,[107]
    Magotty-pie,
My father loves good ale,
    And so do I.

Rowley Powley, pudding and pie,
Kissed the girls and made them cry;
When the girls began to cry,
Rowley Powley runs away.

Rub-a-dub dub,
Three men in a tub;
The butcher, the baker,
The candle-stick maker;
All jumped out of a rotten potato.

St. Dunstan, as the story goes,
Once pulled the Devil by the nose
With red-hot tongs, which made him roar,
That he was heard ten miles or more.

St. Swithin's day, if thou dost rain,[108]
For forty days it will remain:
St. Swithin's day, if thou be fair,
For forty days 'twill rain na mair.

Saw ye aught of my love a-coming from the market?
A peck of meal upon her back,
A babby in her basket;
Saw ye aught of my love coming from the market?

See a pin and pick it up,
All the day you'll have good luck ;
See a pin and let it lay,
Bad luck you'll have all the day !

See, saw, Margery Daw,
Sold her bed and lay upon straw ;
Was not she a dirty slut,
To sell her bed and lie in the dirt ?

See, saw, Margery Daw,
Little Jackey shall have a new master ;
Little Jackey shall have but a penny a day,
Because he can't work any faster.

See, saw, Margery Daw,
The old hen flew over the malt-house ;
She counted her chickens one by one,
Still she missed the little white one,
And this is it, this is it, this is it.

See, saw, sacradown,
Which is the way to London town ?
One foot up, the other foot down,
And that is the way to London town.

See, see! what shall I see?
A horse's head where his tail should be.

———•———

    Shoe the colt,
    Shoe the colt,
  Shoe the wild mare:
    Here a nail,
    There a nail,
  Yet she goes bare.

———•———

Shoe the colt, shoe! [109]
  Shoe the wild mare,
Put a sack on her back,
  See if she'll bear,
If she'll bear
  We'll give her some grains;
If she won't bear,
  We'll dash out her brains!

———•———

Sieve my lady's oatmeal,
  Grind my lady's flour,
Put in a chestnut,
  Let it stand an hour;
One may rush, two may rush,
Come, my girls, walk under the bush.

Simple Simon met a pieman [110]
 Going to the fair;
Says Simple Simon to the pieman,
 "Let me taste your ware."

Says the pieman to Simple Simon,
 "Show me first your penny;"
Says Simple Simon to the pieman,
 "Indeed I have not any."

Simple Simon went a-fishing
 For to catch a whale;
All the water he had got
 Was in his mother's pail.

Simple Simon went to look
 If plums grew on a thistle;
He pricked his fingers very much,
 Which made poor Simon whistle.

—————

Sing, sing! what shall I sing?
The cat has eat the pudding-string!
Do, do! what shall I do?
The cat has bit it quite in two.

—————

Smiling girls, rosy boys,
Come and buy my little toys;

Monkeys made of gingerbread,
And sugar horses painted red.

———

Snail, snail, come out of your hole,[111]
Or else I will beat you as black as a coal.

———

Solomon Grundy,
Born on a Monday,
Christened on Tuesday,
Married on Wednesday,
Took ill on Thursday,
Worse on Friday,
Died on Saturday,
Buried on Sunday:
This is the end
Of Solomon Grundy.

———

Speak when you're spoken to,
Come when one call;
Shut the door after you,
And turn to the wall!

———

Swan swam over the sea —
Swim swan back again.
Well swam swan.

Taffy was a Welshman, Taffy was a thief;[112]
Taffy came to my house and stole a piece of beef:

I went to Taffy's house, Taffy was not at home;
Taffy came to my house and stole a marrow-bone.

I went to Taffy's house, Taffy was in bed,
I took the marrow-bone, and beat about his head.

Tell-tale tit![113]
Your tongue shall be slit,
And all the dogs in town
Shall have a little bit.

Ten and ten and twice eleven,
Take out six and put in seven;
Go to the green and fetch eighteen,
And drop one a-coming.

The barber shaved the mason,
As I suppose
Cut off his nose,
And popped it in a basin.

The cuckoo's a fine bird,
He sings as he flies;

He brings us good tidings,
He tells us no lies.

He sucks little birds' eggs,
To make his voice clear;
And when he sings "cuckoo!"
The summer is near.

———

The lion and the unicorn
Were fighting for the crown:
The lion beat the unicorn
All round about the town.
Some gave them white bread,
And some gave them brown;
Some gave them plum-cake,
And sent them out of town.

———

The girl in the lane, that couldn't speak plain,
Cried, "Gobble, gobble, gobble:"
The man on the hill, that couldn't stand still,
Went hobble, hobble, hobble.

———

The King of France went up the hill, [114]
With twenty thousand men;
The King of France came down the hill,
And ne'er went up again.

8

The man in the moon,
Came down too soon,
To inquire his way to Norwich.
He went by the south,
And burnt his mouth
With eating cold plum-porridge.

The man in the wilderness asked me,[115]
How many strawberries grew in the sea.
I answered him, as I thought good,
As many red herrings as grew in the wood.

The north wind doth blow,
We soon have snow,
And what will poor Robin do then?
    Poor thing!

He'll sit in a barn,
To keep himself warm,
And hide his head under his wing.
    Poor thing.

The pettitoes are little feet,
    And the little feet not big;
Great feet belong to the grunting hog,
    And the pettitoes to the little pig.

The queen of hearts,
  She made some tarts,
All on a summer's day ;
  The knave of hearts,
  He stole those tarts,
And with them ran away :
  The king of hearts
  Called for those tarts,
And beat the knave full sore ;
  The knave of hearts
  Brought back those tarts,
And said he'd ne'er steal more.

  The king of spades
  He kissed the maids,
Which vexed the queen full sore ;
  The queen of spades
  She beat those maids,
And turned them out of door :
  The knave of spades
  Grieved for these jades,
And did for them implore.
  The queen so gent
  She did relent,
And vowed she'd ne'er strike more.

  The king of clubs
  He often drubs
His loving queen and wife ;

The queen of clubs
Returns him snubs,
And all is noise and strife :
The knave of clubs
Gives winks and rubs,
And swears he'll take her part;
For when our kings
Will do such things,
They should be made to smart.

The diamond king
I fain would sing,
And likewise his fair queen;
But that the knave,
A haughty slave,
Must needs step in between :
Good diamond king,
With hempen string,
This haughty knave destroy !
Then may your queen,
With mind serene,
Your royal bed enjoy.

There was a crooked man, and he went a crooked mile,
He found a crooked sixpence against a crooked stile :
He bought a crooked cat, which caught a crooked mouse,
And they all lived together in a little crooked house.

There was a fat man of Bombay,
Who was smoking one sunshiny day,
When a bird, called a snipe,
Flew away with his pipe,
Which vexed the fat man of Bombay.

———·———

There was a girl in our town,[116]
Silk an' satin was her gown,
Silk an' satin, gold an' velvet,
Guess her name, three times I've telled it.

———·———

Tom, Tom, the piper's son,
Stole a pig and away he run!
The pig was eat, and Tom was beat,
And Tom went roaring down the street.

———·———

There was a jolly miller
Lived on the river Dee:
He worked and sung from morn till night,
No lark so blithe as he.
And this the burden of his song
Forever used to be, —
"I jump mejerrime jee!
I care for nobody, — no! not I, ·
Since nobody cares for me."

There was a jolly miller
Lived on the river Dee,
He looked· upon his pillow,
And there he saw a flea,
"O! Mr. Flea,
You have been biting me,
And you must die :"
So he cracked his bones
Upon the stones,
And there he let him lie.

———•———

There was a king, and he had three daughter,
And they all lived in a basin of water ;
The basin bended,
My story's ended.
If the basin had been stronger,
My story would have been longer.

———•———

There was a king met a king
In a narrow lane ;
Says this king to that king,
"Where have you been ? "

O! I've been a hunting
With my dog and my doe.
"Pray lend him to me,
That I may do so."

There's the dog *take* the dog.
" What's the dog's name?"
I've told you already.
" Pray tell me again."

––––•––––

There was a little boy and a little girl
   Lived in an alley ;
Says the little boy to the little girl,
   " Shall I, O! shall I ? "

Says the little girl to the little boy,
   " What shall we do ? "
Says the little boy to the little girl,
   " I will kiss you."

––––•––––

There was a little boy went into a barn,
 And lay down on some hay ;
An owl came out and flew about,
   And the little boy ran away.

––––•––––

There was a little Guinea-pig
Who, being little, was not big,
He always walked upon his feet,
And never fasted when he eat.

When from a place he ran away,
He never at that place did stay ;

And while he ran, as I am told,
He ne'er stood still for young or old.

He often squeaked and sometimes vi'lent,
And when he squeaked he ne'er was silent;
Though ne'er instructed by a cat,
He knew a mouse was not a rat.

One day, as I am certified,
He took a whim and fairly died;
And, as I'm told by men of sense,
He never has been living since.

———•———

There was a little man,[117]
And he wooed a little maid,
And he said, "Little maid, will you wed, wed, wed?
I have little more to say,
Than will you, yea or nay,
For least said is soonest mended-ded, ded, ded."

The little maid replied,
Some say a little sighed,
"But what shall we have for to eat, eat, eat?
Will the love that you're so rich in
Make a fire in the kitchen?
Or the little god of Love turn the spit, spit, spit?"

———•———

There was a little one-eyed gunner
Who killed all the birds that died last summer.

There was a mad man,
And he had a mad wife,
And they lived all in a mad lane!
They had three children all at a birth,
And they too were mad every one.
The father was mad,
The mother was mad,
The children all mad beside;
And upon a mad horse they all of them got,
And madly away did ride.

There was a man, and he had naught,
And robbers came to rob him;
He crept up to the chimney-pot,
And then they thought they had him.

But he got down on t'other side,
And then they could not find him;
He ran fourteen miles in fifteen days,
And never looked behind him.

There was a man of our town,
And he was wondrous wise;
He jumped into a quickset hedge,
And scratched out both his eyes:
And when he saw his eyes were out,
With all his might and main
He jumped into another hedge,
And scratched 'em in again.

There was a man who had no eyes,[118]
He went abroad to view the skies;
He saw a tree with apples on it,
He took no apples off, yet left no apples on it.

———•———

There was a monkey climbed up a tree;[119]
When he fell down, then down fell he.
There was a crow sat on a stone;
When he was gone, then there was none.

There was an old wife did eat an apple;
When she had eat two, she had eat a couple.

There was a horse going to the mill;
When he went on, he stood not still.

There was a butcher cut his thumb;
When it did bleed, then blood did come.

There was a lackey ran a race,
When he ran fast, he ran apace.

There was a cobbler clouting shoon,[120]
When they were mended, they were done.

There was a chandler making candle,
When he them strip, he did them handle.

There was a navy went into Spain,
When it returned, it came again.

There was an old crow [121]
Sat upon a clod ;
There's an end of my song,
That's odd !

———

There was an old couple, and they were poor,
Fa la, fa la la lee !
They lived in a house that had but one door ;
O ! what a poor couple were they.

The old man once he went far from his home,
Fa la, fa la la lee !
The old woman afraid was to stay alone,
O ! what a weak woman was she.

The old man he came home at last,
Fa la, fa la la lee !
And found the windows and door all fast,
"O ! What is the matter ? " quoth he.

"O ! I have been sick since you have been gone,
Fa la, fa la la lee !
If you'd been in the garden you'd heard me groan ; "
"O ! I'm sorry for that," quoth he.

"I have a request to make unto thee ;
Fa la, fa la la lee !
To pluck me an apple from yonder tree ; "
"Ay, that will I, many," quoth he.

The old man tried to get up in the tree,
    Fa la, fa la la lee!
But the ladder it fell, and down tumbled he;
That's cleverly done! said she.

  There was an old man,[122]
  And he had a calf,
   And that's half;
  He took him out of the stall,
  And put him on the wall,
   And that's all.

  There was an old man of Tobago,
  Who lived on rice, gruel, and sago;
  Till, much to his bliss,
  His physician said this, —
  " To a leg, sir, of mutton you may go."

  There was an old woman
   Sold puddings and pies,
  She went to the mill
   And dust flew in her eyes.
  While through the streets,
  To all she meets,
   She ever cries,
   " Hot Pies, — Hot Pies.

There was an old woman[123]
Lived under the hill,
She put a mouse in a bag,
And sent it to the mill;

The miller declared
By the point of his knife,
He never took toll
Of a mouse in his life.

———◆———

There was an old woman[124]
Lived under a hill;
And if she's not gone,
She lives there still.

———◆———

There was an old woman and what do you think?
She lived upon nothing but victuals and drink:
Victuals and drink were the chief of her diet,
And yet this old woman could never be quiet.

———◆———

There was an old woman as I've heard tell,
She went to market her eggs for to sell;
She went to market all on a market-day,
And she fell asleep on the king's highway.

There came by a peddler whose name was Stout,
He cut her petticoats all round about;
He cut her petticoats up to her knees,
Which made the old woman to shiver and freeze.

When this little woman first did wake,
She began to shiver and she began to shake;
She began to wonder and she began to cry,
"O! deary, deary me, this is none of I!"

"But if it be I, as I do hope it be,
I've a little dog at home, and he'll know me;
If it be I, he'll wag his little tail,
And if it be not I, he'll loudly bark and wail."

Home went the little woman all in the dark,
Up got the little dog, and he began to bark;
He began to bark, so she began to cry,
"O! deary, deary me, this is none of I!"

———•———

There was an old woman called Nothing-at-all,
Who rejoiced in a dwelling exceedingly small;
A man stretched his mouth to its utmost extent,
And down at one gulp house and old woman went.

———•———

There was an old woman had nothing,
    And then came thieves to rob her;
When she cried out she made no noise,
    But all the country heard her.

———•———

There was an old woman had three sons,[126]
Jerry, and James, and John:

Jerry was hung, James was drowned,
John was lost and never was found ;
And there was an end of the three sons,
Jerry, and James, and John !

———•———

There was an old woman, her name it was Peg,
Her head was of .wood, and she wore a cork-leg.
The neighbors all pitched her into the water,
Her leg was drowned first, and her head followed a'ter.

———•———

There was an old woman in Surrey,
Who was morn, noon, and night in a hurry ;
Called her husband a fool,
Drove the children to school,
The worrying old woman of Surrey.

———•———

There was an old woman of Leeds,
Who spent all her time in good deeds ;
She worked for the poor
Till her fingers were sore,
This pious old woman of Leeds !

———•———

There was an old woman of Norwich,[127]
Who lived upon nothing but porridge ;
Parading the town,
She turned cloak into gown,
This thrifty old woman of Norwich.

There was an old woman sat spinning,
And that's the first beginning;
  She had a calf,
  And that's half;
She took it by the tail,
And threw it over the wall,
  And that's all.

There was an old woman tossed up in a basket [128]
  Seventy times as high as the moon;
Where she was going I couldn't but ask it,
  For in her hand she carried a broom.

"Old woman, old woman, old woman," quoth I,
  "O whither, O whither, O whither so high?"
"To brush the cobwebs off the sky!
  And I will be back again by and by."

'Twas on a merry time, when Jenny Wren was young,
So neatly as she danced, and so sweetly as she sung, —

Robin Redbreast lost his heart — he was a gallant bird;
He doffed his hat to Jenny, and thus to her he said: —

"My dearest Jenny Wren, if you will but be mine,
You shall dine on cherry-pie, and drink nice currant-wine.

"I'll dress you like a Goldfinch, or like a Peacock gay;
So if you'll have me, Jenny, let us appoint the day."

Jenny blushed behind her fan, and thus declared her mind:
"Then let it be to morrow, Bob; I take your offer kind.

"Cherry-pie is very good; so is currant-wine;
But I will wear my brown gown, and never dress too fine."

Robin rose up early, at the break of day;
He flew to Jenny Wren's house, to sing a roundelay.

He met the Cock and Hen, and bade the Cock declare,
This was his wedding-day with Jenny Wren the fair.

The Cock then blew his horn, to let the neighbors know
This was Robin's wedding-day, and they might see the show.

And first came Parson Rook, with his spectacles and band;
And one of Mother Goose's books he held within his hand.

Then followed him the Lark, for he could sweetly sing;
And he was to be clerk at Cock Robin's wedding.

He sung of Robin's love for little Jenny Wren;
And when he came unto the end, then he began again.

The Bulfinch walked by Robin, and thus to him did say,
"Pray, mark, friend Robin Redbreast, that Goldfinch dressed
      so gay ; —

"What though her gay apparel becomes her very well;
Yet Jenny's modest dress and look must bear away the
      bell!"

Then came the bride and bridegroom; quite plainly was
    she dressed ;
And blushed so much, her cheeks were as red as Robin's
    breast.

But Robin cheered her up; " My pretty Jen," said he,
" We're going to be married, and happy we shall be."

The Goldfinch came on next, to give away the bride ;
The Linnet, being bridesmaid, walked by Jenny's side.

And as she was a-walking, said, " Upon my word,
I think that your Cock Robin is a very pretty bird."

" And will you have her, Robin, to be your wedded wife?"
" Yes, I will," says Robin, " and love her all my life."

" And you will have him, Jenny, your husband now to be?"
" Yes, I will," says Jenny, " and love him heartily."

The Blackbird and the Thrush, and charming Nightingale,
Whose sweet " jug " sweetly echoes through every grove
    and dale ; —

The Sparrow and Tomtit, and many more were there;
All came to see the wedding of Jenny Wren the fair.

" O, then," says Parson Rook, " who gives this maid away?"
" I do," says the Goldfinch, "and her fortune I will pay ; —

"Here's a bag of grain of many sorts, and other things beside;
Now happy be the bridegroom, and happy be the bride!"

Then on her finger fair, Cock Robin put the ring;
"You're married now," says Parson Rook; while the Lark
aloud did sing, —

' Happy be the bridegroom, and happy be the bride!
And may not man, nor bird, nor beast, this happy pair
divide."

The birds were asked to dine; not Jenny's friends alone,
But every pretty songster that had Cock Robin known.

They had a cherry-pie, besides some currant-wine,
And every guest brought something, that sumptuous they
might dine.

Now they all sat or stood, to eat and to drink;
And every one said what he happened to think.

They each took a bumper, and drank to the pair;
Cock Robin the bridegroom, and Jenny Wren the fair.

The dinner things removed, they all began to sing;
And soon they made the place near a mile around to ring.

The concert it was fine; and every bird tried
Who best should sing for Robin, and Jenny Wren the bride.

When in came the Cuckoo, and made a great rout;
He caught hold of Jenny, and pulled her about.

Cock Robin was angry, and so was the Sparrow,
Who fetched in a hurry his bow and his arrow.

His aim then he took, but he took it not right;
His skill was not good, or he shot in a fright;

For the Cuckoo he missed, — but Cock Robin he killed!
And all the birds mourned that his blood was so spilled.

———•———

There was an old woman who lived in a shoe,
She had so many children she didn't know what to do,
She gave them some broth without any bread ;
She whipped them all soundly, and put them to bed.

———•———

There was an owl lived in an oak,
    Wisky, wasky, weedle ;
And every word he ever spoke,
    Was fiddle, faddle, feedle.

A gunner chanced to come that way,
    Wisky, wasky, weedle ;
Says he, "I'll shoot you, silly bird,"
    Fiddle, faddle, feedle.

There were two blackbirds,
   Sitting on a hill,
The one named Jack,
   The other named Jill;
Fly away, Jack!
   Fly away, Jill!
Come again, Jack!
   Come again, Jill!

————

There were two blind men went to see
Two cripples run a race;
The bull did fight the humble-bee,
And scratched him in the face.

————

There were three jovial Welshmen,
   As I have heard them say,
And they would go a-hunting
   Upon St. David's day.[109]

All the day they hunted,
   And nothing could they find,
But a ship a-sailing,
   A-sailing with the wind.

One said it was a ship,
   The other he said, nay;
The third said it was a house,
   With the chimney blown away.

And all the night they hunted,
  And nothing could they find
But the moon a-gliding,
  A-gliding with the wind.

One said it was the moon,
  The other he said, nay;
The third said it was a cheese,
  And half o't cut away.

And all the day they hunted,
  And nothing could they find
But a hedgehog in a bramble-bush,
  And that they left behind.

The first said it was a hedgehog,
  The second he said, nay;
The third it was a pin-cushion,
  · And the pins stuck in wrong way.

And all the night they hunted,
  And nothing could they find
But a hare in a turnip field,
  And that they left behind.

The first said it was a hare,
  The second he said, nay;
The third said it was a calf,
  And the cow had run away.

And all the day they hunted,
  And nothing could they find
But an owl in a holly-tree,
  And that they left behind.

One said it was an owl,
  The other he said, nay ;
The third said 'twas an old man,
  And his beard growing gray.

————

There were three sisters in a hall,[130]
There came a knight amongst them all ;
" Good-morrow, aunt," to the one,
" Good-morrow, aunt," to the other,
" Good-morrow, gentlewoman," to the third.
" If you were my aunt,
  As the other two be,
I would say ' Good-morrow,
  Then, aunts, all three.' "

————

There were two birds sat on a stone,
  Fa, la, la, la, lal, de ;
One flew away, and then there was one,
  Fa, la, la, la, lal, de ;
The other flew after, and then there was none,
  Fa, la, la, la, lal, de ;
And so the poor stone was left all alone,
  Fa, la, la, la, lal, de !

The rose is red, the grass is green;
And in this book my name is seen.

———•———

The rose is red, the grass is green,[181]
Serve Queen Bess, our noble queen;
  Kitty the spinner
  Will sit down to dinner,
And eat the leg of a frog;
  All good people
  Look over the steeple,
And see the cat play with the dog.

———•———

The rose is red, the violet blue,
The gillyflower sweet, — and so are you.
These are the words you bade me say
For a pair of new gloves on Easter-day.

———•———

    The two gray kits,
      And the gray kits' mother,
    All went over
      The bridge together.
    The bridge broke down,
      They all fell in;
  " May the rats go with you,"
      Says Tom Bowlin.

The white dove sat on the castle wall,[182]
I bend my bow and shoot her I shall;
I put her in my glove, both feathers and all;
I laid my bridle upon the shelf,
If you will any more, sing it yourself.

The winds they did blow,
    The leaves they did wag;
Along came a beggar-boy,
    And put me in his bag.

He took me up to London,
    A lady did me buy;
Put me in a silver cage,
    And hung me up on high.

With apples by the fire,
    And nuts for to crack;
Besides a little feather-bed,
    To rest my little back.

They that wash on Monday,
    Have all the week to dry;
They that wash on Tuesday,
    Are not so much awry;
They that wash on Wednesday,
    Are not so much to blame;
They that wash on Thursday,
    Wash for shame;

They that wash on Friday,
  Wash in need ;
And they that wash on Saturday,
  O! they're sluts indeed.

———·———

Thirty days hath September,[133]
April, June, and November ;
February has twenty-eight alone,
All the rest have thirty-one,
Excepting leap-year, that's the time
When February's days are twenty-nine.

———·———

Thirty white horses upon a red hill,[134]
Now they tramp, now they champ, now they stand still.

———·———

1. This is the house that Jack built.[135]

2. This is the malt
    That lay in the house that Jack built.

3. This is the rat,
    That ate the malt
    That lay in the house that Jack built.

4. This is the cat,
    That killed the rat,
    That ate the malt
    That lay in the house that Jack built.

5. This is the dog,
   That worried the cat,
   That killed the rat,
   That ate the malt
   That lay in the house that Jack built.

6. This is the cow with the crumpled horn,
   That tossed the dog,
   That worried the cat,
   That killed the rat,
   That ate the malt
   That lay in the house that Jack built.

7. This is the maiden all forlorn,
   That milked the cow with the crumpled horn,
   That tossed the dog,
   That worried the cat,
   That killed the rat,
   That ate the malt
   That lay in the house that Jack built.

8. This is the man all tattered and torn,
   That kissed the maiden all forlorn,
   That milked the cow with the crumpled horn,
   That tossed the dog,
   That worried the cat,
   That killed the rat,
   That ate the malt
   That lay in the house that Jack built.

9. This is the priest all shaven and shorn,
   That married the man all tattered and torn,
   That kissed the maiden all forlorn,
   That milked the cow with the crumpled horn,
   That tossed the dog,
   That worried the cat,
   That killed the rat,
   That ate the malt,
   That lay in the house that Jack built.

10. This is the cock that crowed in the morn,
    That waked the priest all shaven and shorn,
    That married the man all tattered and torn,
    That kissed the maiden all forlorn,
    That milked the cow with the crumpled horn,
    That tossed the dog,
    That worried the cat,
    That killed the rat,
    That ate the malt
    That lay in the house that Jack built.

11. This is the farmer sowing his corn,
    That kept the cock that crowed in the morn,
    That waked the priest all shaven and shorn,
    That married the man all tattered and torn,
    That kissed the maiden all forlorn,
    That milked the cow with the crumpled horn,
    That tossed the dog,
    That worried the cat,
    That killed the rat,

That ate the malt
That lay in the house that Jack built.

———

Two little dogs were basking in the cinders;
Two little cats were playing in the windows;
When two little mice popped out of a hole,
And up to a fine piece of cheese they stole.
The two little dogs cried, "Cheese is nice!"
But the two little cats jumped down in a trice,
And cracked the bones of the two little mice.

———

This is the key of the kingdom.
In that kingdom there is a city:
In that city there is a town;
In that town there is a street;
In that street there is a lane;
In that lane there is a yard;
In that yard there is a house;
In that house there is a room;
In that room there is a bed;
On that bed there is a basket;
In that basket there are some flowers;
Flowers in the basket, basket in the bed,
Bed in the room, etc., etc.,

———

1. This pig went to market; [146]
2. This pig stayed at home;

3. This pig had a bit of meat ;
4. And this pig had none ;
5. This pig said, " Wee, wee, wee !
   I can't find my way home."

———•———

1. This pig went to the barn ;
2. This ate all the corn ;
3. This said he would tell ;
4. This said he wasn't well ;
5. This went week, week, week, over the door-sill.

———•———

Thomas and Annis met in the dark.
  " Good morning," said Thomas ;
  " Good morning," said Annis ;
And so they began to talk.

" I'll give you," said Thomas.
" Give me ! " said Annis ;
  " I prithee, love, tell me what ? "
" Some nuts," said Thomas.
" Some nuts," said Annis ;
  " Nuts are good to crack."

" I love you," said Thomas.
" Love me ! " said Annis ;
  " I prithee, love, tell me where ? "
" In my heart," said Thomas.
" In your heart ! " said Annis ;
  " How came you to love me there ? "

"I'll marry you," said Thomas.
"Marry me!" said Annis;
   "I prithee, love, tell me when?"
"Next Sunday," said Thomas.
"Next Sunday," said Annis;
   "I wish next Sunday were come."

———

Thomas a Tattamus took two T's,
To tie two tups[136a] to two tall trees;
To frighten the terrible Thomas a Tattamus!
Tell me how many T's there are in all THAT.

———

Three blind mice, see how they run![137]
They all ran after the farmer's wife,
Who cut off their tails with the carving-knife.
Did you ever see such fools in your life?
Three blind mice.

———

Three children sliding on the ice[138]
  Upon a summer's day;
As it fell out, they all fell in,
  The rest they ran away.

Now had these children been at home,
  Or sliding on dry ground,
Ten thousand pounds to one penny
  They had not all been drowned.

You parents all that children have,
　And you that have got none,
If you would have them safe abroad,
　Pray keep them safe at home.

————

Three crooked cripples went through Cripplegate,
And through Cripplegate went three crooked cripples.

————

Three straws on a staff,
Would make a baby cry and laugh.

————

"To bed, to bed," says Sleepy-head ;
　"Let's stay awhile," says Slow ;
"Put on the pot," says Greedy-gut,
　"We'll sup before we go."

————

To make your candles last for aye,
　You wives and maids give ear-o !
To put 'em out's the only way,
　Says honest John Boldero.

————

To market ride the gentlemen,
　So do we, so do we ;
Then comes the country clown,
　Hobbledy gee, Hobbledy gee ;

First go the ladies, nim, nim, nim ;
Next come the gentlemen, trim, trim, trim ;
Then come the country clowns, gallop-a-trot.

———

To market, to market,
　　To buy a plum cake ;
Home again, home again,
　　Ne'er a one baked ;
The baker is dead, and all his men,
And we must go to market again.

———

To market, to market, a gallop, a trot,
To buy some meat to put in the pot ;
Threepence a quarter, a groat a side,
If it hadn't been killed, it must have died.

———

To market, to market, to buy a fat pig,
Home again, home again, dancing a jig ;
Ride to market to buy a fat hog,
Home again, home again, jiggety-jog.

———

To market, to market, to buy a plum bun ; [139]
Home again, home again, market is done.

———

Tom Brown's two little Indian boys,
　　One ran away,

10

The other wouldn't stay, —
Tom Brown's two little Indian boys.

———

Tom he was a piper's son,[140]
He learned to play when he was young;
But all the tune that he could play,
Was, " Over the hills and far away;"
Over the hills, and a great way off,
And the wind will blow my top-knot off.

Now Tom with his pipe made such a noise,
That he pleased both the girls and boys;
And they stopped to hear him play,
  " Over the hills and far away."

Tom with his pipe did play with such skill,
That those who heard him could never keep still;
Whenever they heard they began for to dance,
Even pigs on their hind legs would after him prance.

As Dolly was milking her cow one day,
Tom took out his pipe and began for to play;
So Doll and the cow danced "The Cheshire round,"
Till the pail was broke, and the milk ran on the ground.

He met old Dame Trot with a basket of eggs,
He used his pipe, and she used her legs;
She danced about till the eggs were all broke,
She began for to fret, but he laughed at the joke.

He saw a cross fellow was beating an ass,
Heavy laden with pots, pans, dishes, and glass;
He took out his pipe and played them a tune,
And the jackass's load was lightened full soon.

———·———

Tommy kept a chandler's shop,
Richard went to buy a mop;
Tommy gave him such a knock,
That sent him out of his chandler's shop.

———·———

Tommy Trot, a man of law,
Sold his bed and lay upon straw;
Sold the straw and slept on grass,
To buy his wife a looking-glass.

———·———

Tom shall have a new bonnet,
With blue ribbons to tie on it:
With a hush-a-by and a lull-a-baby,
Who so like to Tommy's daddy?

———·———

Tom, Tom, of Islington,[141]
Married a wife on Sunday;
Brought her home on Monday;
Hired a house on Tuesday;
Fed her well on Wednesday;
Sick was she on Thursday;

Dead was she on Friday;
Sad was Tom on Saturday,
To bury his wife on Sunday.

Trip upon trenchers, and dance upon dishes,
  My mother sent me for some barm, some barm;
She bid me tread lightly, and come again quickly,
  For fear the young men should do me some harm.
Yet didn't you see, yet didn't you see,
What naughty tricks they put upon me?
They broke my pitcher, and spilt my water,
And huffed my mother, and chid her daughter,
  And kissed my sister instead of me.

Tweedle-dum and Tweedle-dee
  Resolved to have a battle,
For Tweedle-dum said Tweedle-dee
  Had spoiled his nice new rattle.
Just then flew by a monstrous crow,
  As big as a tar-barrel,
Which frightened both the heroes so,
  They quite forgot their quarrel.

Twelve pears hanging high,
Twelve knights riding by;
Each knight took a pear,
And yet left eleven there!

Two legs sat upon three legs,[142]
With one leg in his lap;
In comes four legs,
And runs away with one leg.
Up jumps two legs,
Catches up three legs,
Throws it after four legs,
And makes him bring back one leg.

———•———

Two little blackbirds sat upon a hill,
One named Jack, the other named Gill;
Fly away, Jack; fly away Gill;
Come again, Jack; come again Gill.

———•———

Up in the green orchard there is a green tree,
The finest of pippins that ever you see;
The apples are ripe and ready to fall,
And Reuben and Robin shall gather them all.

———•———

Up she goes and down she comes;
If you haven't got apples, I'll give you some plums.

———•———

Upon my word and honor,
As I was going to Bonner,
I met a pig,
Without a wig,
Upon my word and honor.

Up-stairs, down-stairs, upon my lady's window,
There I saw a cup of sack and a race of ginger;
Apples at the fire, and nuts to crack,
A little boy in the cream-pot up to his neck.

Up street, and down street,
    Each window's made of glass;
If you go to Tommy Tickler's house,
    You'll find a pretty lass.

Wash me, and comb me,
And lay me down softly,
And set me on a bank to dry;
That I may look pretty,
When some one comes by.

Wee Willie Winkie
    Runs through the town,
Up-stairs and down-stairs,
    In his night-gown;
Tapping at the window,
    Crying at the lock,
" Are the babes in their bed?
    For it's now ten o'clock."

We're all dry with drinking on't,
We're all dry with drinking on't;

The piper spoke to the fiddler's wife,
And I can't sleep for thinking on't.

———•———

We're all in the dumps,
For diamonds are trumps,
The kittens are gone to St. Paul's!
The babies are bit,
The moon's in a fit,
And the houses are built without walls.

———•———

What are little boys made of, made of?
What are little boys made of?
Snaps and snails, and puppy-dogs' tails;
And that's what little boys are made of, made of.
What are little girls made of?
Sugar and spice, and all that's nice;
And that's what little girls are made of, made of.

———•———

What care I how black I be,
Twenty pounds will marry me;
If twenty won't, forty shall,
I am my mother's bouncing girl!

———•———

What do they call you?
"Patchy Dolly."

Where were you born?
"In the cow's horn."
Where were you bred?
"In the cow's head."
Where will you die?
"In the cow's eye."

————

What is the rhyme for *porringer?* [143]
The king he had a daughter fair,
And gave the Prince of Orange her.

————

What's the news of the day,
Good neighbor, I pray?
"They say the balloon
Is gone up to the moon.'

————

What shoemaker makes shoes without leather, [144]
With all the four elements put together?
Fire and water, earth and air;
Every customer has two pair.

————

When a twister a-twisting, will twist him a twist, [145]
For the twisting his twist, he three times doth intwist;
But if one of the twines of the twist do untwist,
The twine that untwisteth, untwisteth the twist.

Untwirling the twine that untwisteth between,
He twists, with the twister, the two in a twine;
Then twice having twisted the twines of the twine,
He twisteth the twine he had twined in twain.

The twain that, in twining, before in the twine,
As twines were intwisted, he now doth untwine;
'Twixt the twain intertwisting a twine more between,
He, twirling his twister, makes a twist of the twine.

When good King Arthur ruled this land,
  He was a goodly king;
He stole three pecks of barley-meal,
  To make a bag-pudding.

A bag-pudding the king did make,
  And stuffed it well with plums:
And in it put great lumps of fat,
  As big as my two thumbs.

The king and queen did eat thereof,
  And noblemen beside;
And what they could not eat that night
  The queen next morning fried.

When I was a little boy, I lived by myself,
And all the bread and cheese I got I put upon the shelf;

The rats and the mice did lead me such a life,
I was forced to go to London to buy me a wife.

The streets were so broad, and the lanes were so narrow,
I could not get my wife home without a wheelbarrow;
The wheelbarrow broke, my wife got a fall,
Down tumbled wheelbarrow, little wife, and all.

When I was a little boy, I had but little wit,
It is some time ago, and I've no more yet;
Nor ever, ever shall, until that I die,
For the longer I live, the more fool am I.

When I was a little girl, I washed my mammy's dishes;[146]
Now I am a great girl, I roll in golden riches.

When I was a little boy, my mother kept me in;
Now I am a great boy, and fit to serve the king;
I can handle a musket, I can smoke a pipe,
I can kiss a pretty girl at ten o'clock at night.

When I was a little girl, about seven years old,
I hadn't got a petticoat, to cover me from the cold;
So I went into Darlington, that pretty little town,
And there I bought a petticoat, a cloak, and a gown,

I went into the woods and built me a kirk,
And all the birds of the air, they helped me to work ;
The Hawk, with his long claws, pulled down the stone,
The Dove, with her rough bill, brought me them home ;
The Parrot was the clergyman, the Peacock was the clerk,
The Bulfinch played the organ, and we made merry work.

———+———

When I went up Sandy Hill,
    I met a sandy boy;
I cut his throat, I sucked his blood,
    And left his skin a hanging-o.

———+———

When the wind is in the east,
'Tis neither good for man nor beast;
When the wind is in the north,
The skillful fisher goes not forth;
When the wind is in the south,
It blows the bait in the fishes' mouth;
When the wind is in the west,
 Then 'tis at the very best.

———+———

When V and I together meet,
They make the number Six complete.
When I with V doth meet once more,
Then 'tis they Two can make but Four.
And when that V from I is gone,
Alas! poor I can make but One.

Where are you going, my pretty maid?
" I'm going a-milking, sir," she said.
May I go with you, my pretty maid?
" You're kindly welcome, sir," she said.
What is your father, my pretty maid?
" My father's a farmer, sir," she said.

Say, will you marry me, my pretty maid?
" Yes, if you please, kind sir," she said.
Will you be constant, my pretty maid?
" That I can't promise you, sir," she said.
Then I won't marry you, my pretty maid!
" Nobody asked you, sir!" she said.

———•———

Where have you been all the day,[147]
        My boy, Willy?
" I've been all the day,
  Courting of a lady gay;
  But O! she's too young
  To be taken from her mammy."

What work can she do,
        My boy, Willy?
Can she bake and can she brew,
        My boy, Willy?

She can brew and she can bake,
And she can make our wedding-cake;
But O! she's too young
To be taken from her mammy.

What age may she be?
What age may she be?
        My boy, Willy?
"Twice two, twice seven,
Twice ten, twice eleven ;
But O! she's too young
To be taken from her mammy."

———

Who comes here?[118]
  "A grenadier."
What do you want?
  "A pot of beer."
Where is your money?
  "I've forgot."
Get you gone,
  You drunken sot!

———

Who ever saw a rabbit
Dressed in a riding habit,
Gallop off to see her friends, in this style?
I should not be surprised
If my lady is capsized,
Before she has ridden half a mile.

———

Who killed Cock Robin?
  "I," said the Sparrow,
  "With my bow and arrow,
I killed Cock Robin.

Who saw him die?
  "I," said the Fly,
  "With my little eye,
And I saw him die."

Who caught his blood?
  "I," said the Fish,
  "With my little dish,
And I caught his blood."

Who made his shroud?
  "I," said the Beadle,
  "With my little needle,
And I made his shroud."

Who shall dig his grave?
  "I," said the Owl,
  "With my spade and showl,"
And I'll dig his grave."

Who'll be the parson?
  "I," said the Rook,
  "With my little book,
And I'll be the parson."

Who'll be the clerk?
  "I," said the Lark,
  "If it's not in the dark,
And I'll be the clerk."

Who'll carry him to the grave?
  "I," said the Kite,
  "If 'tis not in the night,
And I'll carry him to his grave."

Who'll carry the link?
  "I," said the Linnet,
  "I'll fetch it in a minute,
And I'll carry the link."

Who'll be the chief mourner?
  "I," said the Dove,
  "I mourn for my love,
And I'll be chief mourner."

Who'll bear the pall?
  "We," said the Wren,
    Both the cock and the hen,
"And we'll bear the pall."

Who'll sing a psalm?
  "I," said the Thrush,
    As she sat in a bush,
"And I'll sing a psalm."

And who'll toll the bell?
  "I," said the Bull,
  "Because I can pull;"
And so, Cock Robin, farewell.

All the birds in the air
  Fell to sighing and sobbing,
   When they heard the bell toll
For poor Cock Robin.

———•———

William and Mary, and George and Anne,
Four such children had never a man;
They put their father to flight and shame,
And called their brother a shocking bad name.

———•———

Willy boy, Willy boy, where are you going?
  I'll go with you, if I may.
'I'm going to the meadow to see them a-mowing,
  I'm going to help them make hay."

———•———

  Willy, Willy Wilkin,
  Kissed the maids a-milking,
      Fa, la, la!
  And with his merry daffing,
  He set them all a-laughing,
      Ha, ha, ha!

———•———

Young Roger came tapping at Dolly's window,
    Thumpaty, thumpaty, thump!
He asked for admittance, she answered him "No.
    Frumpaty, frumpaty, frump!

" No, no, Roger, no! as you came you may go!"
Stumpaty, stumpaty, stump!

———•———

You shall have an apple,
You shall have a plum,
You shall have a rattle basket,
When your dad comes home.

Baa, Baa, Black Sheep.

Baa, baa, black sheep, have you a-ny wool? Yes, kind sir, three bags full,—

One for my master, one for my dame, But none for the lit-tle boy that lives in the lane.

Ding Dong Bell.

Ding dong bell, pussy's in the well: Who put her in ? Lit-tle John-ny Green. Who pulled her out ? Big

John - ny Stout. What a naught-y boy was that to drown poor pus - sy cat,

Who nev-er did him a - ny harm, but killed the mice in his fa-ther's barn.

Bobby Shafto.

Allegretto.

Bob-by Shaf-to's gone to sea, Sil - ver buck - les on his knee; He 'll come back and

mar - ry me, — Pret-ty Bob - by Shaf - to. Bob- by Shaf-to's fat and fair, Comb-ing down his

yel - low hair: He 's my love for ev - er - more, — Pret - ty Bob - by Shaf - to.

Bless you, Burnie Bee.

Andantino.

Bless you, bless you, Burnie Bee! Tell me where my true love be, Be she east, or be she west,

Seek the path that she loves best; Go and whisper in her ear That I ever think of her, Tell her all I

have to say Is about our wedding-day; Burnie Bee, no lon-ger stay, Take your wings and fly a-way.

Little Bo-peep.

Lit - tle Bo - peep has lost her sheep, and can't tell

where to find them. Leave them a - lone, and they'll come home, and

bring their tails be - hind them, and bring their tails be - hind them.

Tom, Tom of Islington.

Tom, Tom of Is-ling ton, Mar-ried a wife on Sun-day, Brought her home on Mon-day,

Hired a house on Tues-day, Fed her well on Wednes-day, Sick she was on Thurs-day,

Dead was she on Fri-day, Sad was Tom on Sat-ur-day, To bu-ry his wife on Sun-day.

Jack and Jill.

Jack and Jill went up the hill, To fetch a pail of wa - ter; Jack fell down and

broke his crown, And Jill came tumbling af - - ter. Ho - la! ho - la!

Ho - la! ho - la! Jack fell down and broke his crown, And Jill came tumbling af - ter.

We'll go to the Woods.

1. We'll go to the woods, says Richard to Rob-in; We'll go to the woods, says Rob-in to Bob-in; We'll go to the woods, says John all a-lone; We'll go to the woods, says ev'ry one.

"To Bed, to Bed, says Sleepy Head."

To bed,   to bed,   says Sleep - y   Head;   Let's stay a - while, says

Slow,   Let's stay a - while, says Slow;   Put on   the pot,   says Greedy.

Gut,   We'll sup be - fore we go,   We'll sup be - fore we go.

NOTES.

Note **1**, page 2. — *A carrion crow sat on an oak.* This song, under a somewhat different form, is of the time of Charles I. It was discovered by Mr. Halliwell in MS. Sloane 1489, fol. 17.

2, p. 3. — *Tocher.* Dowry. A Scottish word.

3, p. 5. — *A duck and a drake.* These lines, which refer to the amusement of water-skimming, are probably of considerable antiquity. In Higgins's translation of Junius's "Nomenclator" (8°, London, 1585, p. 299), the word *epostracismus* is thus defined : " A kind of sport or play with an oister shell or stone thrown into the water, and making circles yer it sink. It is called *a duck and a drake, and a halfe-penie cake.*"

4, p. 12. — *A man of words and not of deeds.* The earliest known version of this song occurs in MS. Harl. 1927, of the time of James I.

5, p. 12. — *A riddle, a riddle, as I suppose.* A cinder-sifter.

6, p. 12. — *Arthur O'Bower has broken his band.* A storm of wind.

7, p. 12. — *As I walked by myself.* A song on King William the Third.

8, p. 13. — *As I was going over London bridge.* Gloves.

9, p. 13. — *As I was going o'er London bridge.* A firebrand with sparks on it.

10, p. 14. — *As I was going o'er Tipple Tine.* A swarm of bees.

11, p. 15. — *As I went through the garden gap.* A cherry.

12, p. 16. — *As round as an apple, as deep as a cup.* A well.

13, p. 16. — *As soft as silk, as white as milk.* A walnut.

14, p. 16. — *As titty-mouse sat in the witty to spin.* *Titty mouse* is an old English name for the bird called a titmouse. *Tit* or *titty* means small or diminutive, and *mouse* in this word has no connection with the name of the familiar rodent so called, but comes from a different root, the Anglo-Saxon *mâse*, Old High German *meisa, meisâ,* and is allied to *mew* in *seamew.* *Witty* is the name given in Shropshire to the mountain ash.

15, p. 17. — *At Dover Dwells George Brown, Esquire.* This couplet is intended to impress on the memory the dominical letters annexed in some calendars to the first days of the several months.

16, p. 17. — *Awa', birds, away !* The song of a little boy while passing his hour of solitude in a cornfield.

17, p. 18. — *A was an apple-pie.* This "nursery romance" is at least two centuries old. Dr. John Eachard, in a work entitled "Observations upon the Answer to an Enquiry into the Grounds and Occasions of the Contempt of the Clergy," published by him in 1671, refers to it by way of illustration. "Whereas," he says, "it has been observed that some of our clergie are sometimes over nice in taking notice of the meer words that they find in texts, so these [the English Papists of his time] are so accurate as to go to the very *letters.* As suppose, sir, you are to give an exhortation to repentance upon that of St. Matthew, 'Repent ye, for the kingdom of Heaven is at hand:' you must observe that Repent is a rich word, wherein every letter exhorts us as to our duty,— Repent, R readily, E earnestly, P presently, E effectually, N nationally, T thoroughly. Again, Repent Roaringly, Eagerly, Plentifully, Heavily (because of *h*),* Notably, Terribly. And why not, Repent Rarely, Evenly, Prettily, Elegantly, Neatly, Tightly? And also, why not, A apple-pasty, B bak'd it, C cut it, D divided it, E eat it, F fought for it, G got it, etc. I had not time, sir, to look any further into their way of preaching; but if I had, I am sure I should have found that they have no reason to despise our church upon that account." *Page* 160.

18, p. 19. — *Bobby Shafto's gone to sea.* This is the common version, but in another form of the rhyme Wooley Foster is the swain. In the latter half of the last century there was a real Robert Shafto, who was popularly called "Bonny Bobby Shafto." The family to which he belonged was of great antiquity in the north of England. He resided at Whitworth, county of Durham, and his portrait represents him as very young-and handsome, and with *yellow* hair. He was at one time a member of Parliament. A Miss Bellasyse, known as the heiress of Brance-peth, is said to have died for love of him. He married Miss Anne Duncombe, April 18, 1794, and died November 24, 1797.

19, p. 19. — *A was an archer, and shot at a frog.* This is called Tom Thumb's Alphabet.

20, p. 19. —*Bouse.* To drink. An old cant term.

21, p. 20. — *Marry.* An interjection which is supposed to be a corruption of the name of the Virgin Mary.

22, p. 20. — *Barnaby Bright he was a sharp cur.* The name of Barnaby Bright occurs in an old proverb:—

> "Barnaby Bright,
> The longest day, and the shortest night,"—

which refers to Saint Barnabas's day, June 11. Before the change of style, this was the day of the summer solstice.

23, p. 20. — *Clerk.* In England this word is pronounced *klark*, and is a perfect rhyme to "bark."

24, p. 21. — *Betsy Bell and Mary Gray.* These were two celebrated beauties,

* That is, because the *h* is silent. Eachard pronounced the word *'eavily.*

daughters of two country gentlemen who resided in the neighborhood of Perth. When the plague of 1666 broke out in that vicinity, they retired into solitude, to avoid infection, and built themselves a bower in a secluded spot called Burn Brae, on a small streamlet tributary to the Almond. There they lived together, being supplied with food and other necessaries by a young man whom they both tenderly loved. After a time he unwittingly caught and communicated to them the fatal contagion, of which they all three soon died.

25, p. 21. — *Black within, and red without.* A chimney.

26, p. 21. — *Black we are, but much admired.* Coals.

27, p. 21. — *Bless you, bless you, burnie bee.* Burnie bee is a name given in the north of England to the ladybird. The lines are said by children when they throw the insect into the air, to make it take flight. Variations of the song are current throughout the north of Europe. One of them, set to music, is given on page 165.

28, p. 22. — *Buff says Buff to all his men.* These lines are used in a game, being repeated by one child who holds a wand to the face of others in succession, making grimaces and causing them to laugh, for doing which they have to pay a forfeit.

29, p. 22. — *Bryan O'Lin, and his wife, and wife's mother.* These lines, slightly altered, are to be found, according to Halliwell, in a little black-letter book by W. Wager, printed about the year 1560, entitled "A very mery and pythie commedie, called, the longer thou livest, the more foole thou art." In Ritson's "North Country Chorister," Durham, 1802, p. 1, there is a whole song ending thus: —

> "Tommy Linn, and his wife, and his wife's mother,
> They all fell into the fire together;
> They that lay undermost got a hot skin:
> We are not enough, says Tommy Linn."

30, p. 23. — *Buz, quoth the blue fly.* This song occurs in Ben Jonson's "Masque of Oberon."

30a, p. 23. — *Bunting.* An old term of endearment.

31, p. 25. — *Hey! diddle, diddle.* In Preston's "Lamentable Tragedie, containing the Life of Cambises, king of Percia," — written about 1561, and reproduced by Hawkins in the first volume of his "Origin of the English Drama, Oxford, 1763, — one of the characters, called Ambidexter, says: —

> "They be at hand, sir, with stick and fidle;
> They can play a new dance called, *Hey, diddle, diddle!*"

Halliwell suggests that the nursery rhyme may have been originally an adaptation to that dance-tune.

32, p. 25. — *Come, butter, come.* An old charm to make butter form in the churn. It was to be said thrice.

33, p. 26. — *Crowdy.* To fiddle. *Crowd* is an old name for a fiddle; a *crowder* was a fiddler. The passage, trivial as it is, will recall to the minds of some that fine saying of Sir Philip Sidney, in his " Defence of Poesy " : " I never heard the old song of Percy and Douglas, that I found not my heart moved more than with a trumpet ; and yet it is sung but by some blind *crowder*, with no rougher voice than rude style."

34, p. 27. — *A gown of silk and a silver tee.* A *tee* is doubtless a corruption of the archaic or provincial word *dee*, meaning *a thimble*, from the French *dé*.

35, p. 34. — *Eggs, butter, bread.* A puzzle or exercise on the slate.

36, p. 34. — *Elizabeth, Elspeth, Betsey, and Bess.* As Elspeth, Betsey, and Bess are merely diminutives of Elizabeth, the answer to the riddle is easy.

37, p. 34. — *Every lady in this land.* Correct the punctuation, and the assertion will be seen to be " true without deceit."

38, p. 34. — *Eye winker.* Lines said to a very young child, the parts of the face named being touched as the lines are repeated, and the chin, when reached, being playfully struck upward, so that the tongue may be gently bitten.

39, p. 35. — *F for fig, J for jig.* As I and J are, or were formerly considered to be, one and the same letter, the explanation of the rhyme is evidently the word FINIS (FJNJS).

40, p. 35. — *Father Iohnson, Nicholas Iohnson's Son.* The initials of the words in these lines taken forwards and backwards, form the word *Finis*. On reaching the end of a book, boys have a practice of repeating the couplet, or they say that they have got to Father Johnson.

41, p. 35. — *Flour of England, fruit of Spain.* A plum-pudding.

42, p. 36. — *Gay go up and gay go down.* This is a game rhyme. A number of children form a ring and pass between two others (raised a little above them), who make an arch by extending their arms and taking hold of each other's hands One of the ring is suddenly taken captive by the lowering of their arms, and is then privately asked whether he will have *oranges* or *lemons* (names applied to themselves by the two who form the arch, they having previously agreed which designation shall belong to each), and he goes behind the one he may chance to name, which is also done privately. When all are thus divided into two parties, they conclude the game by trying to pull each other beyond a certain line.

43, p. 37. — *Some she ate, and some she shod.* Shod is an old or provincial preterit of *shed*, and means spilt.

44, p. 38. — *Girls and boys, come out to play.* The antiquity of this rhyme is established by a very curious ballad, written about the year 1720, which is given by Halliwell in his " Popular Rhymes and Nursery Tales," p. 21. The same authority states that the tune to this song may be found " in all the late editions of Playford's ' Dancing Master.' "

44a, p. 40. — *Great A was alarmed' at B's bad behavior.* " The proper tune is that to ' Unfortunate Miss Bailey.' " R. W. Dixon, in " Notes and Queries," March 1, 1856.

45, p. 40. — *And O dear me.* This exclamation is thought to be a corruption of the Italian *O Dio mio*, O my God.

46, p. 41. — *He that would thrive.* These lines are from Benjamin Franklin's "Poor Richard's Almanac."

47, p. 43. — *Sing a song of sixpence.* This verse is quoted in Beaumont and Fletcher's "Bonduca," act v. sc. 2. In Shakespeare's "Twelfth Night," act ii. sc. 2, Sir Toby Belch says: "Come on ; there is sixpence for you ; let's have a song," — which is thought to be an allusion to this nursery rhyme. In old times it was a favorite device to introduce live birds into pies, after they were baked, so that when they were cut up the birds might fly out.

48, p. 44. — *Hick-a-more, Hack-a-more.* Sunshine.

49, p. 44. — *Hickery, dickery, 6 and 7.* This rhyme is used in the operation of "counting out," which is a very important one in many childish games. The children stand in a row, and the operator begins with the rhyme, appropriating a word to each, till he comes to the person who receives the last word, and who is accordingly "out." The process is repeated till there is only one left, who by virtue of that fact becomes the hero of the game, whatever it may be.

50, p. 45. — *Higgledy, piggledy.* Currants.

51, p. 46. — *How many miles is it to Babylon?* This is a dialogue game played in a manner very similar to that of "Gay go up, and gay go down" (see note 42), the last of the ring being taken captive — if possible.

52, p. 47. — *Humpty Dumpty sat on a wall.* An egg.

53, p. 49. — *If ifs and ands.* Said when any one indulges much in supposition.

54, p. 51. — *I had a little husband.* This nursery ballad probably celebrates a part of the history of Tom Thumb, who is thought to have been of mythological origin — one of the dwarfs of Scandinavian faith. He was, at a later day, placed among the knights at King Arthur's court, where he is said to have performed "many maruailous acts of manhood." According to popular tradition, he was buried in the cathedral at Lincoln, where a little blue flag-stone in the pavement was long shown as his monument ; but it has been displaced and lost.

55, p. 52. — *Moppet.* That is, a little girl.

56, p. 52. — *I had a little nut-tree.* This may refer to Joanna of Castile, who visited the court of Henry VII. in 1506.

57, p. 53. — *I have a little sister, they call her Peep, Peep.* A star.

58, p. 54. — *Infir taris.* Divide each word into two parts, and the sense will be brought out. In repeating the piece, — which has been traced to the time of Henry VI., — the words are to be run together and pronounced so quickly that it cannot be told whether they are English or gibberish.

59, p. 55. — *In marble walls as white as milk.* An egg.

60, p. 55. — *Intery, mintery, cutery, corn.* A counting-out rhyme. *See* note 49.

12

61, p. 55. — *I saw a peacock with a fiery tail.* The lines are intentionally punctuated falsely.

62, p. 57. — *Lugs.* Ears. A Scottish and North of England term.

63, p. 58. — *I went into my grandmother's garden.* A tobacco-pipe.

64, p. 59. — *I went to the toad that lies under the wall.* These lines, with a very slight variation, are found in Ben Jonson's "Masque of Queens."

65, p. 59. — *I went to the wood and got it.* A thorn.

66, p. 61. — *Jack Sprat could eat no fat.* This rhyme has been current for more than two centuries. In the earliest known version, the hero and heroine were no less exalted personages than "Archdeacon Pratt and Joan his wife." In their more modern form, the lines form the beginning of a tale which is largely a mere cento of well-known nursery jingles.

67, p. 62. — *Jim and George were two great lords.* Halliwell suggests that King George and the Pretender may be alluded to in these lines. To *girn* is to grin; also, to cry as a child, which is the meaning in this place.

67a, p. 63. — *Jenny Wren.* "The Christian names given to birds deserve a notice. Thus we have Jack Snipe, Jenny Wren, Jack Daw, Tom Tit, Robin Redbreast, Poll Parrot, Jill Hooter, Jack Curlew, Jack Nicker, and King Harry for the goldfinch; and the list might be widely extended. A starling is always Jacob, a sparrow is Philip, a raven is Ralph [a magpie is Madge], and the consort of the Tom Tit rejoices in the euphonic name of Betty! Children give the name of Dick to all small birds, which, in nursery parlance, are universally Dicky-birds." — *Halliwell.* Several of the names here mentioned are unknown in America.

68, p. 66. — *Lavender blue and rosemary green.* These verses are said to be connected with the amusements of Twelfth Night. They probably refer to the choosing the king and queen. The following version is given for the sake of adding the traditional tune to which it was sung.

Lav - en - der blue, fid - dle fad - dle, Lav - en - der green,

When I am king, fid - dle fad - dle, You shall be queen,

Call up your men, fid - dle fad - dle, Set them to work,

Some with a rake, fid - dle fad dle, Some with a fork,

Some to make hay, fid - dle fad - dle, Some to the farm,

Whilst you and I, fid - dle fad - dle, Keep our - selves warm.

69, p. 66. — *Rock.* A sort of distaff. The term is obsolete.

70, p. 67. — *Let us go to the wood, says this pig.* A game with the five toes, each toe being touched in succession as the lines are repeated.

71, p. 67. — *Little Bo-peep has lost her sheep.* The game of bo-peep, in which children hide from each other, and cry —

> Bo-peep, little Bo-peep,
> Now's the time for hide and seek, —

is of great antiquity, and is not infrequently referred to by our old writers. Another and simpler game bearing the same name, is that in which a nurse puts something over the head of an infant for an instant, and then removes it quickly, saying, as she does so, Bo-peep. The term appears to have been connected at a very early period with sheep.

72, p. 69. — *Little General Monk.* The reference is to George Monk, Duke of Albemarle (b. 1608, d. 1670), distinguished as a parliamentarian general during the time of the Commonwealth and the Protectorate, and still more noted for the part he took in bringing about the restoration of the Stuarts.

73, p. 70. — *Little Jack Horner sat in a corner.* The rhyme of Jack Horner is only a fragment of an extended chap-book tale in verse, entitled "The Pleasant History of Jack Horner, containing his witty Tricks and pleasant Pranks, which he plaied from his Youth to his riper Years." A copy of this history, embellished with frightful wood-cuts, is preserved in the Bodleian Library. It is reproduced in the Notes to the first edition of Halliwell's "Nursery Rhymes of England," printed as a part of the Percy Society's Publications. The story is founded on that of "The Fryer and the Boy," 12mo, London, 1617, and both are taken from the more ancient tale of "Jack and his Stepdame," which has been published by Mr. Wright. The traditional lines differ somewhat from those in the chap-book, in which Jack is represented as not only the hero but the author of the rhyme.

> "When friends they did together meet,
> To pass away the time —
> Why, little Jack, he sure would eat
> His Christmas pie in rhyme.
> And said, 'Jack Horner, in the corner,
> Eats good Christmas pie,
> And with his thumbs pulls out the plums,
> And said, Good boy am I.'"

74, p. 70. — *And went to Wigan to woo.* Wigan is a town on the river Douglas, county of Lancaster.

75, p. 70. — *When he came to a beck.* A beck is a rivulet or small brook.

76, p. 72. — *Sat on a tuffett.* *Tuffett* is a diminutive of *tuff*, a provincial English form of *tuft*.

77, p. 72. — *Little Nancy Etticoat.* A candle.

78, p. 75. — *Lives in winter.* An icicle.

79, p. 76. — *Long legs, crooked thighs.* A pair of tongs.

80, p. 77. — *Make three-fourths of a cross.* TOBACCO.

81, p. 77. — *Matthew, Mark, Luke, and John.* A charm formerly much used by children instead of a prayer. There are many variations of it. See for a number of such, taken down from the lips of children in the dioceses of Worcester and Salisbury, a " Report on the state of parochial education in the Diocese of Worcester," by the Rev. E. Field, printed as an appendix to the National Society's report for 1841. Ady, in his " Candle in the Dark," London, 1656, p. 58, gives the first two lines as having been used in the time of Queen Mary. The origin of the lines is perhaps to be found in the " Enchiridion Leonis Papæ," first published at Rome in 1532, and early translated into French. This work consists of a collection of prayers, for the most part burlesqued or disfigured and adopted as charms to avert or heal diseases. One of them, entitled " Paternôtre blanche, pour aller infailliblement en paradis," contains this sentence ; " Au soir m'allant coucher, je trouvis trois Anges à mon lit couchés, un aux pieds, deux au chevet, la bonne Vierge Marie au milieu," etc.

82, p. 78. — *Mistress Mary quite contra'ry.* *Contrary* was formerly always accented on the second syllable. Thus Milton says, —

> " Fame, if not double-faced, is double-mouthed,
> And with *contra'ry* blast proclaims most deeds."

83, p. 78. — *She loved coffee, and I loved tea.* Tea was introduced into England in 1657. Ten years later it became a regular article of import, and, according to Macaulay, " was soon consumed in such quantities that financiers began to consider it a fit subject for taxation." The word was for a long time pronounced *tay*, as it is by other European nations. Pope, who died in 1744, so pronounced it, as is indicated by the following lines : —

> " Here thou, great Anna, whom three realms *obey*,
> Dost sometimes counsel take, and sometimes *tea*."

This nursery-rhyme cannot, therefore, — at least in its present form, — be of any great antiquity.

84, p. 79. — *Multiplication is vexation.* These lines were found, a few years ago, in a manuscript dated 1570.

85, p. 81. — *My father was a Frenchman.* A game rhyme. One child holds out his arm, and another, in illustration of the third and fourth lines, strikes him lightly with the side of his hand first at the shoulder and then at the wrist; and then, at the word "middle," with some force on the muscles at the elbow-joint, so as suddenly to bend the arm.

86, p. 82. — *My true love lives far from me.* Several versions of this metrical riddle are common in the north of England. One of them, beginning "I had four brothers over the sea," is given on page 53.

87, p. 84. — *Nose, nose, jolly red nose.* These lines are found in Ravenscroft's "Deuteromelia, or the second Part of Musickes Melodie," 1609, song No. 7.

88, p. 85. — *Of all the gay birds that e'er I did see.* Part of an old song, the whole of which is to be found in "Deuteromelia."

89, p. 85. — *O, where are you going.* This pretty ballad "appears," says Halliwell, "to be a humorous imitation of an Elizabethan eclogue-song. Its style guarantees its antiquity."

90, p. 86. — *Old King Cole.* Cole, Coël, or Coilus, was a legendary British prince who flourished, according to the old chroniclers, about the middle of the third century after Christ. Assuming independence, he attacked and took possession of the Roman colony at Camelodunum, which he named after himself Colechester, that is, *Cole castrum*, or Cole's camp. The Roman general Constantius Chlorus endeavored to regain the place, and immediately laid siege to it. This lasted for three years, when, having seen Helena, Cole's daughter, who is described as being very beautiful, he made peace with Cole, on condition of receiving Helena in marriage. This was agreed to, and it is asserted that Constantine the Great was the fruit of their union. At Colchester there is a large earthwork, — probably the remains of a Roman amphitheatre, — which is popularly called "King Cole's Kitchen."

91, p. 87. — *Old Mother Goose.* This is merely a modern versification and amplification of the fable, attributed to Æsop, entitled Ὄρνις χρυσοτόκος, or the Goose that laid the Golden Egg. The following is a free translation of it: "A certain man had the good fortune to possess a goose that laid him a golden egg every day. But dissatisfied with so slow an income, and thinking to seize the whole treasure at once, he killed the goose; and, cutting her open, found her — just what any other goose would be."

92, p. 8·. — *Old Mother Hubbard.* The antiquity of this tale is established by the rhyme of *laughing* to *coffin* in the third stanza. The word was formerly pronounced *loffing*, and was so spelt. Halliwell says that "the first three verses are all the original. The rest is modern, and was added when 'Mother Hubbard' was the first of a series of eighteen-penny books published by Harris."

93, p. 92. — *Old Mother Twitchett had but one eye.* A needle and thread.

94, p. 94. — *One-ery, two-ery, hickary, hum.* A counting out rhyme used by children to decide who shall begin a game. *See* note 49.

95, p. 94 — *One-ery, two-ery.* Another rhyme used for the same purpose. A similar one is found in Swedish.

96, p. 94. — *One misty, moisty morning.* A somewhat different version is given in D'Urfey's "Wit and Mirth, or Pills to Purge Melancholy," 1719, vol. iv. page 148. *Moisty* for *moist,* is found in "Mirror for Magistrates," and other old books.

97, p. 95. — *One moonshiny night.* The story on which this rhyme is founded is related by Matthew Paris.

98, p. 96. — *One to make ready.* Used by school-boys when two are starting to run a race.

99, p. 99. — *Over the water, and over the lea.* The allusion is to King Charles II., the "merry monarch."

100, p. 99. — *Pease-pudding hot.* A game with the hands.

101, p. 101. — *Please to remember.* This song commemorates the attempt of Guy Fawkes and his fellow-conspirators to blow up the King and Parliament on the 5th of November, 1606.

102, p. 101. — *Peter White will ne'er go right.* This is quoted by Parkin in his reply to Dr. Stukeley's second number of the "Origines Roystonianæ," 1748, p. vi. Halliwell says, "I am not aware that it is still current." It is, however, well known in the American nursery.

103, p. 102. — *Poor Old Robinson Crusoe.* A fragment of a song introduced by Russell in the character of Jerry Sneak, in Foote's farce, "The Mayor of Garatt."

104, p. 104. — *Ring the bell.* A play with the face. Sometimes the following variation is used : —

> "Brow brinky,
> Eye winky,
> Chin choppy,
> Nose noppy,
> Cheek cherry,
> Mouth merry,"

each feature mentioned being tapped as the lines are repeated.

105, p. 105. — *Three wise men of Gotham.* Gotham is a parish in Nottinghamshire, England. It has long been celebrated for the remarkable stupidity imputed to the inhabitants. They are said to have heard the cuckoo once upon a time, and on discovering that the notes — which were new and strange to them — came from a certain bush, proceeded to hedge it in, in order to prevent the bird from making her escape. A bush is still shown on an eminence about a mile south of the village which is called the "Cuckoo bush." It is not the original one, but is said to be planted on the site of that. "Men in all ages," says Fuller, "have made them selves merry with singling out some place, and fixing the staple of stupidity and stolidity therein. So the Phrygians in Asia, the Abderitæ in Thrace, and Bœotians in Greece, were notorious for dulmen and blockheads. These places, thus slighted and scoffed at, afforded some as witty and wise persons as the world produced. So Democritus was an Abderite, Plutarch a Bœotian, &c. . . . As for Gotham, it doth breed as wise people as any which causelessly laugh at their simplicity."

106, p. 105. — *Here a nail, and there a prod. Prod* is a provincial English term for an iron pin, such as are fixed in pattens.

107, p. 106. — *Round about, round about.* This rhyme must be of considerable antiquity, as *magotty-pie* or *magot-pie* is an old name for a *magpie.* The word is found in the dictionaries of Hollyband (1593), Cotgrave (1611), and Minsheu (1617) Shakespeare uses it in Macbeth : —

> "Augurs, and understood relations, have
> By *magot-pies*, and choughs and rooks brought forth
> The secret'st blood of men." *Act* iv. *Sc.* 4.

The first syllable of *magpie* is *Mag*, the diminutive of Margaret, given as a sobriquet to the pie (Lat. *pica*), that black and white bird to which so much quaint superstition has always attached. *Marget* and *maggot* were formerly in use as other contractions of the same name.

108, p. 107. — *St. Swithin's day, if thou dost rain.* It is an old belief, that, if it rains on St. Swithin's day (July 15), it will rain more or less for forty days following. St. Swithin — born about 800, and died about 862 — was Bishop of Winchester, and tutor to King Alfred. According to the common tradition, which, however, rests on not the slightest basis of fact, he gave directions on his death-bed that he should be buried in the church-yard on the north side of the minster, under the droppings from the eaves, and when the monks, in violation of his wishes, attempted to place his remains under the chancel, he testified his displeasure by miraculously causing a heavy rain of forty days' continuance. Hence the popular superstition.

109, p. 109. — *Shoe the colt, shoe!* These lines are used in a play with the toes. There are many versions of the song in English, and it is also found in Danish.

110, p. 110. — *Simple Simon met a pieman.* The popular tale of Simple Simon is one of early and unknown authorship. It is of considerable length, and forms a chap-book, but the verses here given are all that are generally recited in the nursery.

111, p. 111. — *Snail, snail, come out of your hole.* This is a boy's invocation to a snail to come out of the little chamber it so curiously hollows out in limestone for its residence.

112, p. 112. — *Taffy was a Welshman, Taffy was a thief.* This is a tale for the 1st of March. St. David, renowned as one of the Seven Champions of Christendom, is the patron saint of Wales. His feast is on the 1st of March, and is the national holiday. *Taffy* is a Welsh mispronunciation of *Davy*, or *Davvy*, a diminutive of David, which is naturally enough one of the most popular and common of Welsh names. Hence, *Taffy* has become a nickname for a Welshman, or for the Welsh collectively, just as *Sawney* (a diminutive of Alexander) has for the Scotch.

113, p. 112. — *Tell-tale, tit.* Said by children in derogation of an informer A common variation of the first line is

"Liar, liar, lick spit."

This is found, with merely the slight variation of "dish" for "spit," in Chettle's "Tragedy of Hoffman, or a Revenge for a Father," London, 1631.

114, p. 113. — *The King of France went up the hill.* In a tract, called "Pigges Corantoe, or Newes from the North," 4to, London, 1642, page 3, this is called "Old Tarlton's Song." Richard Tarleton was an actor contemporary with Shakespeare, and was famous for playing the clown in his plays, and in those of others. He died in the year 1588. A common variation is the following : —

> "The King of France marched up the hill,
>   With twenty thousand men,
> And when he got them up the hill,
>   He marched them down again."

115, p. 114. — *The man in the wilderness asked me.* This is found in a MS. of the 17th century, in the Sloane Collection.

116, p. 117. — *There was a girl in our town.* Ann.

117, p. 120. — *There was a little man.* This is a part of a little work called "Authentic Memoirs of the Little Man and the Little Maid, with some interesting Particulars of their Lives." Halliwell thinks that it is more modern than the verses here given.

118, p. 122. — *There was a man who had no eyes.* He had one eye, and the tree had two apples on it.

119, p. 122. — *There was a monkey climbed up a tree.* These verses were written in 1626, against the Duke of Buckingham

120, p. 122. — *Clouting shoon.* *Shoon* is the old plural of *shoe.* Clouted shoes were shoes of which the soles were fortified with nails.

121. p. 123. — *There was an old crow.* An ancient Suffolk song for a bad singer.

122, p. 124. — *There was an old man.* A song very similar to this is current in Sweden. See Arwidsson, "Svenska Fornsånger," iii. 488.

123, p. 125. — *There was an old woman.* The first two lines are the beginning of a song in D'Urfey's "Pills to Purge Melancholy," vol. v. p. 13.

124, p. 125. — *There was an old woman.* These lines form part of an old catch, printed in the "Academy of Complements," ed. 1714, p. 108.

125, p. 125. — *There was an old woman, as I've heard tell.* This nursery-ballad is found in one form or another in most countries in Europe.

126, p. 126. — *There was an old woman had three sons.* These lines are a modern version of a part of an old catch found in the " Academy of Complements " (p. 140) referred to above.

127, p. 127. — *There was an old woman of Norwich.* In America, *Norwich* is usually pronounced as it is spelt. In England, it forms a perfect rhyme to " porridge."

128, p. 128. — *There was an old woman tossed up in a basket.* This is supposed to be the original song of " Lilliburlero, or Old Woman, whither so high ? " the tune to which was published in 1678.

129, p. 133. — *Upon St. David's day.* March 1. See note 112.

130, p. 135. — *There were three sisters in a hall.* From MS. Sloane, 1489, fol. 16, written in the time of Charles I.

131, p. 136. — *The rose is red, the grass is green.* The tune to which these lines were formerly sung may be found in " The English Dancing Master," 1651, p. 37.

132, p. 137. — *The white dove sat on the castle wall.* From a play by W. Wager, called " The longer thou livest, the more foole thou art," London, 4to.

133, p. 138. — *Thirty days hath September.* These mnemonic lines occur, with slight variations, in an old play, called " The Returne from Parnassus," London, 1606, 4to.

134, p. 138. — *Thirty white horses upon a red hill.* The teeth and gums.

135, p. 138. — *This is the house that Jack built.* The original of this accumulative story is a Chaldaic hymn in *Sepher Haggadah*, fol. 23, a translation of which, with an historical interpretation by P. N. Lebericht, is given by Halliwell in his " Nursery Rhymes of England," 6th ed., London, p. 288.

136, p. 141. — *This pig went to market.* A song set to the five toes or the five fingers.

136 a, p. 143. — *To tie two tups to two tall trees.* *Tup* is a provincial English name for a ram.

137, p. 143. — *Three blind mice, see how they run.* The original of this ditty is to be found in Ravenscroft's " Deuteromelia," London, 1609, 4to, where the music is also given.

138, p. 143. — *Three children sliding on the ice.* These lines are to be found in their primitive form in " The Loves of Hero and Leander," London, 1653. They form part of a rambling story, in doggerel rhymes, no less than eighty-four lines in length. From the concluding verse of the story, as told in the original, it should seem that these lines were composed in the early part of the civil wars of Charles I.

139, p. 145. — *To market, to market, to buy a plum bun.* This is partially quoted in Florio's " New World of Words," 1611, under the word Abimba.

140, p. 146. — *Tom he was a piper's son.* Part of this is in a song called Jockey's Lamentation," in D'Urfey's "Pills to Purge Melancholy," 1719, vol. v p. 317.

141, p. 147. — *Tom, Tom, of Islington.* In Poor Robin's Almanac for 1693 is the following passage which may furnish us with the original of this celebrated ballad, though the latter buried his troublesome wife on Sunday: "How one saw a lady on the Saturday, married her on the Sunday, she was brought to bed on the Monday, the child christened on the Tuesday, it died on the Wednesday, was buried on the Thursday, the bride's portion was paid on the Friday, and the bridegroom ran clear away on the Saturday!" Compare also the very similar history of Solomon Grundy, given on p. 112.

142, p. 149. — *Two legs sat upon three legs.* Two legs is a man; three legs, a stool; one leg, a leg of mutton; four legs, a dog. This riddle, together with several others current at the present day, are contained in a collection formed early in the 17th century by Randle Holmes, the Chester antiquary, which is preserved in MS. Harl. 1962.

143, p. 152. — *What is the rhyme for porringer?* Written on occasion of the marriage of Mary, daughter of James, Duke of York, afterwards James II., with William, Prince of Orange. The song from which these lines are taken is given in "The Jacobite Minstrelsy," Glasgow, 1828, p. 28.

144, p. 152. — *What shoemaker makes shoes without leather.* A horse-shoer.

145, p. 152. — *When a twister a-twisting will twist him a twist.* This is said to be a certain cure for the hiccough, if repeated without stopping to take breath. It is to be found in Dr. Wallis's " Grammatica Linguæ Anglicanæ," Oxford, 1674, p. 164.

146, p. 154. — *When I was a little girl, I washed my mammy's dishes.* This is given by Aubrey in MS. Lansd., 231.

147, p. 156. — *Where have you been all the day.* This is a very popular nursery ballad. There is a Scottish version of it, called "Tammy's Courtship," which is given by Halliwell in his "Popular Rhymes and Nursery Tales," p. 260.

148, p. 157. — *Who comes here?* This ditty is more than a hundred and fifty years old. It is referred to in a ballad entitled "Namby Pamby, or a Panegyric on the New Versification," which was written about the year 1720. See note 44.

149, p. 158. — *With my spade and showl. Showl* is an archaic form of *shovel.*

150, p. 160. — *William and Mary, George and Anne.* This rhyme alludes to William III. and George, Prince of Denmark, husband of Queen Anne.

www.ingramcontent.com/pod-product-compliance
Lightning Source LLC
Chambersburg PA
CBHW030323270326
41926CB00010B/1476